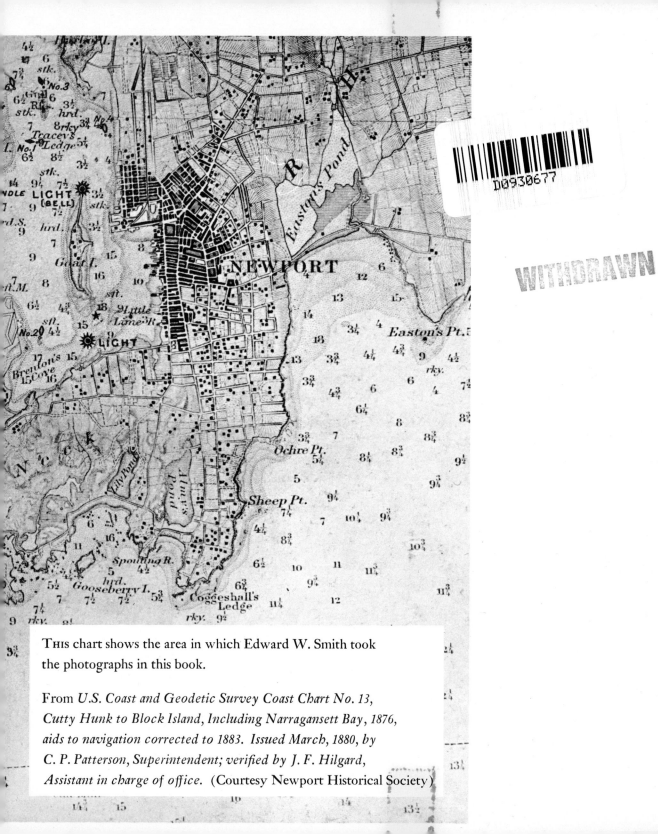

THIS chart shows the area in which Edward W. Smith took the photographs in this book.

From *U.S. Coast and Geodetic Survey Coast Chart No. 13, Cutty Hunk to Block Island, Including Narragansett Bay, 1876, aids to navigation corrected to 1883. Issued March, 1880, by C. P. Patterson, Superintendent; verified by J. F. Hilgard, Assistant in charge of office.* (Courtesy Newport Historical Society)

*Workaday Schooners*

# Workaday Schooners

The Edward W. Smith Photographs

taken on Narragansett Bay, 1895-1905;

Together with Writings and Plans Describing

the Designs and Use of Schooners of the Period

*Compiled by* EDWARD W. SMITH, JR.

*International Marine Publishing Company* / CAMDEN, MAINE

The compiler and the publisher wish to thank the Marine Historical Association, Mystic, Connecticut, custodian of the Edward W. Smith Collection, for permission to publish the pictures in this book.

# TO MY WIFE

*Who has made this possible*

# CONTENTS

*The view from 64 Washington Street, Newport, Rhode Island, in 1894. It was this stimulus that made Edward Smith take his camera sailing with him.*

# PREFACE

IT WAS A TREAT TO HAVE MY FATHER SHOW ME HIS SCHOONER PICTURES. They were in a huge album which he would place across his knees and leaf through, a page at a time, as I, sitting beside him, peered over his elbow. The album contained scores of four-by-five photographs reproduced on blue print paper in distinctive, unforgettable hues.

The schooners represented adventure in an exciting, vanished world, and I would eagerly question him about them. He always answered me patiently, telling a little about each vessel with a smile, for, though he seemed to enjoy remembering the days of sail, he made it clear to me that they were gone and would never return. I can hear him now saying of the pictures. "They will never be worth a thing to anyone."

It didn't matter what he said, the pictures were wonderful in my eyes, and the fact that my father knew so much about the schooners placed him in my highest esteem. From them, my approach to the sea, to sailing, to tides, buoys, rocks, channels, harbors, docks, wind, rigging, waves, anchors, and clouds was as through the eyes of a schooner captain. Though my feelings for these things have tempered with age, the pictures have survived unchanged, and in going back over them, I still get a tinge of excitement.

My father was born in Germantown, Pennsylvania, in 1875. His natural skill in sciences and mechanics led to his earning the first degree in chemical engineering granted by the University of Pennsylvania. His interests were broader than chemistry and engineering, for besides being a photographer, he did pioneering work in aviation, and he won a prize in 1908 for powered flight with a model plane of his own design. He worked at the Electric Storage Battery Company for all his life, and his patents were instrumental in the development of storage batteries. He made operational model steamboats as a hobby.

Father was a direct descendent of Thomas Robinson of Newport, who, in colonial times, built the house which still stands at 64 Washington Street. In May, when school was out, my father's family moved from Germantown to Newport to spend the summer. This annual pilgrimage required travel by train to New York and then by Fall River Line steamer to Newport.

Life revolved about the sea at 64 Washington Street, and everyone knew how to swim and how to row. The family sailboat, a little catboat called the *Kingfisher* built locally· by the famous Button Swan, was used almost exclusively in the early years by my father's older brother, Bill, and his two sisters. In 1885, when he graduated from Harvard, Bill was given the big keel catboat *Falcon*. This left the *Kingfisher* free for my father, and it was probably not long afterward that he learned to sail.

In long vacations from law school, Bill was on board the *Falcon* nearly all the time. He sailed frequently to the Vineyard and occasionally to Maine. He owned a camera before 1890 and took pictures of what he saw on his cruises. His plates were very flat and are difficult to print now. As nearly as I can determine, Plate 11 and the first photograph in Part II were taken by him.

On July 4, 1892, while off Brenton's Reef on a sail around Aquidneck Island, the *Falcon* was caught in a bad squall, capsized, and sank. Both Bill and his friend, Ned Stewardson, were drowned. My father was saved, drifting ashore on the *Falcon's* removable bowsprit, which his brother had given him just as the boat went down. This accident was the talk of all Narragansett Bay at the time. It was the dominant event in my father's entire life.

*The photographer, Edward W. Smith, sailing the* Kingfisher I *about 1894. He took the pictures in this book from this boat and from the* Kingfisher II. *The first* Kingfisher *was built by Button Swan in 1872.*

The family did not come back to Newport until 1894. The majority of photographs in this book were taken after this date.

My father had a large box camera fitted with a spring shutter. This, he explained to me, was a real improvement over the shutter on his brother's camera, which had required a quick flick of the finger to pass the aperture across the lens and expose a plate.

Newport teemed with marine traffic. Though there were plenty of steamboats around, and railroads were well established, they were reserved for passengers and fast freight. Cheap, bulky cargoes were carried by schooner. In addition to workaday vessels, Newport harbored the ostentatious yachts of millionaires, for it was a watering place for high society.

My father, a straight-laced Quaker, was most prejudiced against the showy rich and would not photograph their yachts. Instead, he focused his camera on the commercial and fishing schooners which were everywhere and which were taken for granted. His prejudices evidently were very unusual, for although numerous collections of yachting photographs from this period are available, photographs of small, working schooners such as these are only rarely seen.

The *Kingfisher* was replaced by the *Kingfisher II* in 1897, and it was from this later catboat that most of the pictures were taken. I don't believe any of the pictures were made after 1905, for it was then that my mother came on the scene, and they soon had a large family. My father was a quiet, gentle man, loved and respected by all who knew him. He died in Germantown in 1940.

The four-by-five glass plates were stacked in a heavy wooden box that was put in a closet in our house in Germantown. When the household was broken up in 1955, I told my sister, Sarah A. G. Smith, that no one would ever bother to reprint the plates and that they should be destroyed. She said nothing but kept

*The* Kingfisher II *tied up at her dock with the lighthouse on the north end of Goat Island in the background. She was built in 1896 by Thomas Stoddard at the "Point" section in Newport not far from the Smith summer home. Now owned by Edward W. Smith's grandson, John E. Benson, she was sailed until 1970 from a mooring off No. 64 Washington Street.*

them quietly, and then gave them back to me thirteen years later, when I thought differently.

I enlarged them all myself during the winter of 1968. It was a most stimulating job, and I got tremendous satisfaction watching pleasing scenes and forgotten vessels emerge on the paper as each print developed.

Interest in the completed collection has matched my early enthusiasm, and I have given the plates to the Marine Historical Association at Mystic, Connecticut, to make them available to everyone.

My father was apparently more interested in the photographer's ability to record what he sees than he was in preserving details of the schooners themselves. He left few written records, and identification of the vessels has been difficult and, in many cases, impossible. Fortunately, to look at these schooners is to be challenged as to their identity, and, one by one, many have been identified. Some of these beautiful vessels, however, must always remain unnamed.

The finished captions, many times revised, contain opinion, speculation, and conjecture as well as fact; they are, by their very nature, controversial both in language and in content. They make no pretense of being the final word.

To answer questions which the pictures may raise in the minds of inquisitive readers, three classic writings are included in the book. Howard I. Chapelle's description of the evolution of the Gloucester schooner was written in 1936. G. Browne Goode, in his 1884 report to the government on the fishing industry, gives a detailed description of mackerel catching from the schooners. Charles S. Morgan, in a 1963 article, gives a historian's description of the New England coasting trade. In addition, a story by John T. Rowland tells what it was like to sail a large schooner.

Though this book has an obvious appeal to the maritime historian, it is to yachtsmen that I hope it will be of greatest interest. For a modern yachtsman, sailing into Narragansett Bay with other sails all around, will probably have forgotten that he is following in a long tradition. To leaf through these pages is to look back and see what he would have seen seventy-five years ago. The pictures show that the Bay, then too, was dotted with sails.

The schooners were a rugged lot. Wood, hemp, cotton, and tar were used to build them, and they represented the development of improvements made by generations of skilled shipbuilders. Their beauty and seakindliness are striking, and it may be a surprise to realize that could we sail past one today, there would be much about the shape of her hull and the cut of her sails that we could talk about with familiarity.

The book presents a marvelously able looking fleet of vessels and bears testament to the skill and ability of our forefathers. We have good reason to be proud of our heritage.

Those readers familiar with Narragansett Bay will recognize that the pictures were all taken between the old Lightship and Rose Island, in a body of water about five miles long, with a width ranging up to about two miles. One picture, Plate 59, was taken at Vineyard Haven.

At least one of the schooners, the *Altana M. Jagger* (Plate 73), lived until I appeared. I have snapshots of her taken in 1932 with a reef eliminating a rip in her mainsail, drifting down the Bay. Later that summer, she was lost on the beach near Watch Hill, Rhode Island. I played in her wreck and remember being surprised that her hold, apparently intact, was filled with sand. It didn't occur to me until recently that she had probably carried in to the beach, instead of to Providence, her destination, a cargo of Long Island sand.

The late John F. Leavitt of Mystic Seaport gave me great help and encouragement. I wish that he could have seen these pictures published. I want to thank Roger C. Taylor of International Marine Publishing Company, who, interested from the beginning, has been instrumental in following through the identification of these schooners. He has called on other authorities including Captain W. J. L. Parker, Captain Gordon Thomas, Captain Francis E. Bowker, and Albert M. Barnes for many identifications. My thanks go to these men for the part they have taken in making this work as authentic as possible.

EDWARD W. SMITH, JR.

Darien, Connecticut
October, 1974

# PART I

# *Fishing Schooners*

*Then the jaws of the booms whined against the masts, and the sheets creaked, and the sails filled with roaring; and when she slid into a hollow she trampled like a woman tripped in her own silk dress, and came out, her jib wet half-way up, . . .*
*from Rudyard Kipling's* Captain's Courageous

PLATE 1.   A little fellow eases out into the swell.  With his dory stowed on deck and his sails hanging limp, the helmsman hunches over his wheel, perhaps hoping for a little more breeze.


*Preceding page.* Mackerel seiners off Beavertail, waiting for the afternoon breeze.

PLATE 2. The *Venus* of Gloucester bound out with a nice northwester. She was built at Kennebunk, Maine, in 1877. Though at 12.41 gross tons and 11.83 net tons, she is certainly a small fishing schooner, she has all the features of one of her larger sisters. Note her anchors, stowed flukes outboard.

PLATE 3. *(opposite)*. The *Nellie* of Gloucester coming in. She was built at Tiverton, Rhode Island, in 1878. Equipped to catch more than one kind of fish, she has a harpoon slung across her swordfishing pulpit, and a couple of dories handy at the stern. Note the bonnet on the jib and the gaskets hanging ready on the main boom. Her plumb stem was unusual.

PLATE 4. Becalmed in the East Passage. In addition to schooners, many small fishing boats were rigged as sloops. This one has sent down her topmast. The bonnet has been unlaced from her jib and stopped off beneath it; the jib also has a reef which could be used in heavy going. The double-ender she is towing looks to be a small, short-ended version of a seine boat. This fellow's lot seems enviable; it's a nice afternoon and he has left all his cares ashore to go off fishing in a good boat.

PLATE 5. Running in wing-and-wing. The schooner's progress softens an already light breeze. The man at the tiller has no protection from the sun, but the Skipper has taken partial refuge in the companionway. The two men forward have the coolest spot on board and are probably scrutinizing the yacht beating out past them.

PLATE 6.   The *Annie Pitcher*, a small, double-ended fishing sloop lying peacefully alongside.  Note her plank bowsprit and the way the pulpit has been bent out to let a harpooner lean way forward.  Though her skipper has not bothered to attach deadeyes to the shrouds, he has purchased a new set of halyard cleats which he has attached directly to the mast.  She has a large fish hold amidships.  Noticeable too are her galvanized pump and her circular iron traveler built to accommodate the tiller from her outboard rudder.  She has a casual air about her, and the scull hole in her obviously home-made skiff makes one guess that her skipper may be a veteran fisherman.

PLATE 7. A Gloucester sloop boat reaching in past Fort Adams. Not as well known a type as the schooners, these boats were developed in the Eighties after a depression had forced schooner owners to go to smaller vessels. This was probably one of the smaller sloop boats; they ranged from 40 feet to 60 feet long. The crew is forward watching the harbor unfold and ready to get the headsails off.

PLATE 8. The *Edith Bean* reaching in with a bone in her teeth. She was built at Camden, Maine, in 1877 and was registered in Boston. Her tonnage was 17.22 gross. She was 46.4 feet long, with a beam of 15.2 feet, and a depth of 5.5 feet. Note the jib downhaul and curve in the foreboom.

PLATE 9. The same schooner running in dead before it. Note that the bonnet has been taken off her jib.

PLATE 10.   The *Mary A. Brown* of Harwich, Massachusetts, with two catboats, taking advantage of a northeast breeze to reach out past Castle Hill Light. They are keeping in close to the rocks to stay out of a foul tide. The *Brown* was built at Bath, Maine, in 1876. Her tonnage was 15.65, net 14.87. She was 41.8 feet long, with a beam of 13.6 feet and a depth of 5.1 feet. In 1896 she was registered in Dennis, Massachusetts, was owned by Mary A. Snow of West Harwich, and was captained by Freeman R. Berry. Her record tells of getting ashore four times, on Block Island on October 26, 1897 and January 14, 1898, on Negro Island Bar, Maine, on August 30, 1900, and at Great Boars Head, New Hampshire, on December 5, 1900. On the first three groundings, she was floated off without damage, but on the last stranding she was lost with her crew of five.

PLATE 11.  The *Hattie S. Clark* becalmed off Fort Adams.  She was built at Essex, Massachusetts, in 1866, and hailed from Gloucester, where she was owned by J. O. Proctor, Jr.  Note the long wooden anchor stock.  A typical "sharpshooter," she had plenty of sail (see text, page 114).  There is a permanent foot-rope rigged on the end of her long, main boom.  She foundered in a squall off Frying Pan Shoals, North Carolina, in 1890.  Five men were lost.

PLATE 12.   Seven schooners putting to sea at noonday.  The smaller schooners happen to have their staysails outside the foregaff, while the big fellows down to leeward have them set inside.  They are moving along nicely in a light breeze.

PLATE 13.  A sharpshooter boiling along past the prominent "Horsehead" tower. Though her bluff bow turns up quite a fuss, she leaves little wake.  The stain on the mainsail came from tarred shrouds.  Galvanized wire rigging was introduced later.  Note the fenders at her main rigging for taking the seine boat alongside.

PLATE 14. *(opposite)*.  The same schooner looks quite different returning into the harbor on a southwest breeze.  The crew is taking it easy and will have little work till she gets into the harbor.

PLATE 15.   Surging ahead on a fresh puff. Booms and seine boat are lifting; there's no holding her back.

PLATE 16. *(opposite, top)*.   A mackerel seiner running in past Castle Hill Light with her seine boat in tow astern. These vessels chased mackerel from the Virginia Capes to Newfoundland. Each could carry about 100 barrels of fish in brine. (For a description of mackerel seining vessels and operations, see page 131.) With not enough wind to keep the booms out, the crew may be impatient to make port. She looks a big, able vessel.

PLATE 17. *(opposite, bottom)*.   The *John Feeney* fetches in on a northwester. She was 65 feet long on deck, 58.5 feet at the waterline, with a beam of 19.5 feet, and a draft of 9.5 feet. (See plan, page 186.) She had a live fish well fitted amidships. She was built in 1885 at Noank, Connecticut, by John Latham and Son, and was registered in Stonington, Connecticut, before being sold to a New York owner. She was manned by a captain and eleven hands. She fished for blues between Fire Island and Delaware Bay from April to October, and the rest of the year went codfishing between the coast of Maryland and Block Island. No one has bothered to shift her main topsail, as it will soon be taken in. The *Feeney* was one of a very small number of these schooners built with round sterns.

PLATE 18. The *Eddie Davidson* coming in past Beavertail hard on a northeast wind. Her tonnage was 82 gross, 77 net. She was 78.8 feet long, with a 23.1 foot beam, and a depth of 7.7 feet. She was built at Boothbay, Maine, in 1883, and owned at Wellfleet, Massachusetts. She was sold to T. A. Langsford of Gloucester in 1892, and was sold to Newfoundland in 1899. Lucky is the man on the quarter watching her go.

PLATE 19. The *Laura E. Gamage* running out with a clear northwester. She was built at Bristol, Maine, in 1877 and was registered at Newport, Rhode Island. Her tonnage was 13.21 gross. She was 39 feet long, with a beam of 13.5 feet, and a depth of 5.5 feet. Note the balls at the topmast heads and the slack foretopmast backstay, or "freshwater stay." Even on such a nice summer morning, the man at the wheel may be looking forward to jibing over, so the mainsail will stop cutting off his sun.

PLATE 20. Easing up by Newport Light on Goat Island. Note the topsail clewline rove through bullseyes on the leech of the sail. There are oilskins drying on the fore boom. This schooner is probably the *Horace Albert*, built in Bath, Maine, in 1880. In 1896, she was registered in Gloucester. Her gross tonnage was 68.70. She was 73 feet long, with a beam of 21.5 feet, and a depth of 7.6 feet. The schooner, the catboat under her bowsprit, and the tug, with her fancy carved eagle atop the wheelhouse, show the tempo of life in these times. The tower belongs to St. John's Church.

PLATE 21.  Working in against a northeasterly breeze.  The Skipper appears to be waving to the vessel on his weather bow; he'll have a hard time getting close enough to hail her.

PLATE 22. *(opposite).*    The *Lucy W. Dyer* overtaking a little fellow. She was built at Bath, Maine, in 1884, and was owned in Portland. Her tonnage was 82 gross, 72 net. She was 82.8 feet long, with a beam of 22.6 feet and a depth of 7.9 feet.  She stranded and was lost in 1891; her crew was saved.

PLATE 23.    Two schooners fetching out with a light westerly. The fellow up ahead has even eased off a little.  Note the clew earings rove off for the first and second reefs on the near schooner. The third one was left off, since the cringle was further inboard, and so the earing could be passed relatively easily.  The dory and seine boat have been hove right up short while leaving the harbor, but perhaps presently will be let further astern.

PLATE 25. *(opposite)*. Running in dead before it with the main boom squared off and the foresail and headsails blanketed. This view shows how the seine boat "outrigger" was rigged.

PLATE 26. The *Alice*, followed by another fishing schooner, coming down the
Bay in a grey easterly. She is also the schooner seen bows-on at the far left
of the half-title page of this book. She was built at Bath, Maine, in 1876 and
hailed from Provincetown in the 1890's. Her tonnage was 85.06. She was 83.9
feet long, with a beam of 22.8 feet, and a depth of 8.2 feet. Her first two
seasons out, she was highliner of the New England mackerel seining fleet,
netting 3,000 barrels in 1876 and 1,400 barrels in 1877. In 1880, she caught
3,700 barrels, worth $19,548. In 1881, 4,905 barrels worth $28,055. On May 16,
1881, off Block Island, she caught 30,000 mackerel. She made two voyages to
the Cape of Good Hope seeking mackerel in the winters of 1889-90 and 1890-91.
On the first trip, her master, Josiah A. Chase, found fish and had good luck
with hook and line, on one occasion taking 100 barrels in four days. On the
second trip, however, the *Alice* encountered a gale that carried away her fore
rigging and split the mainsail. Nor had she seen fish up to that time. In this
view, the main topsail has been taken in, and the crew on deck is standing
ready to take the rest of the sail off her when she rounds up in Newport Harbor.

PLATE 27.  The *Stowell Sherman* sailing out close-hauled.  She was built at Essex, Massachusetts, in 1876 by Charles O. and Samuel Story.  Her gross tonnage was 92.49, net 87.87.  She was 83 feet long, with a beam of 23 feet, and a depth of 8.2 feet.  She is recorded as having arrived at Provincetown on October 16, 1893 with 110 barrels of mackerel, making a total catch for that season of 1,025 barrels.  She is a "clipper schooner," typical of those built in the 1860's and 1870's.  The clippers had long, hollow waterlines and carried lots of sail.  Though they were quite fast, their high rig was dangerous and many vessels were lost. (See text, page 119).  The *Sherman* has a nicely setting suit of sails and seems to be moving well for the amount of breeze.

PLATE 28.   The *Hattie and Lottie* beating in against a light breeze. She was built by Moses Adams at Essex, Massachusetts, in 1884, and was owned by J. P. Edwards in Dennis, Massachusetts in 1894. Her gross tonnage was 101.44; net, 96.37; she was 85 feet long, with a 22.6-foot beam, and a depth of 8.7 feet. She was registered in Providence, Rhode Island, from 1904 to 1907, whence she sailed in the Cape Verde Island trade under the Portuguese flag as the *Maria de Soledad*.

PLATE 29. Becalmed off Rose Island.

PLATE 30. *(opposite).* The *Oliver Wendell Holmes* reaching in on a dry southeaster. She was built by Willard Burnham at Essex, Massachusetts, in 1890 for W. H. Jordan of Gloucester. She stranded in fog and was lost on Seal Island, Nova Scotia, on December 30th, 1901. The crew made it ashore and were saved.

PLATE 31. A pair of schooners ghosting in. The seine boats have been pulled alongside and made fast to the outriggers to keep them clear. These forty-footers were heavier than their relatives, the whaleboats, but still had fine lines (see text, page 134). Seine nets were kept in them ever ready for a school of fish. They were towed astern in all but the roughest weather, when it was a real chore to get them in on deck.

PLATE 32. A fine example of a "clipper" schooner sailing full-and-by. Note that the jibboom runs out along the port side of the bowsprit.

PLATE 33. The *Marguerite Haskins*, as smart a fishing schooner as any, standing in past Horsehead with a bone in her teeth to envy. She was built by Tarr and James at Essex, Massachusetts, in 1893, from a design by George M. McClain of Rockport. Her gross tonnage was 101, net 72. She was 92.4 feet long, with a beam of 24.8 feet, and a depth of 9.4 feet. She was sold into the Cape Verdes trade in 1923. The *Haskins* is a good example of the yacht-like fishing schooners popular in the 1890's, sometimes called "Fredonia" schooners, after the original *Fredonia* designed in 1889 by Edward Burgess, the great yacht designer. The hull is narrower and deeper than the "clipper;" the lines are finer, with less bulky bows and quarters; and jibboom and flying jib have been eliminated. These later schooners had greater ultimate stability than the "clippers" (see text, page 127 and plan, page 187.)

PLATE 34.   With her anchor catted and her forestaysail aback, this big seiner is just getting underweigh. Most of the crew is still standing by; one fellow is perched on the rail right above the hawse where the anchor hangs.  Beneath a certain shabbiness, she looks a finely proportioned vessel.

PLATE 35. *(opposite).*   Heading offshore in a smokey sou'wester.  The coaster, just visible over the dory, will be astern and to leeward before long.  The fishing schooner's seine boat is towing astern, out of the picture; the outrigger for towing it alongside is visible just above the lee bow wave.

PLATE 36.  Bucking a foul tide off Castle Hill in company with a sloop and a catboat. She may have just jibed over, for the jib is still trimmed to weather.

PLATE 37. *(opposite)*.  The *Hattie M. Graham* on the wind with all her topsails set. She was built by Moses Adams at Essex in 1891 for Tom Hodge and Captain Joe Graham of Gloucester. She was named for the Captain's daughter. Her tonnage was 140.59 gross and 133.57 net. She was 108.2 feet long, 24.3 feet in beam, and had a depth of 11 feet. She stranded and was lost in Banbine Cove, Cape Breton, in 1909. The crew were saved. Note the whisker to spread the bowsprit shroud, the boom tackle rove off on the main boom for use off the wind, the single row of reef points in the mainsail, and the lines at the main top for the mastheadman, whose job was to shift over the topsail. Note also the tripline rigged to the freshwater stay used to shift the fore topsail halyard up over the stay when resetting the sail on a new tack.

PLATE 38. Everything is hung up to try to get her in, but the breeze just hasn't much strength. The photographer's boat has evidently attracted the attention of the crew; perhaps the big schooner is having trouble catching his little catboat in the light air.

PLATE 39. Trying to run wing-and-wing in a small breeze. Perhaps it will "make" a little and push her on in. Note the evidence of chafe by the main peak halyard blocks on the topsail.

PLATE 40.  The *Harvard* outward bound on a close reach.  She was built in 1891 by John James of Essex for W. H. Jordan of Gloucester.  Her tonnage was 112 gross, 76 net.  She was 95.4 feet long, 23.6 feet in beam, with a depth of 10.4 feet.  (See plan, page 188.)  After an active career in several fisheries, she was sold for rumrunning in March, 1927.  Later that year, she was seized by the Coast Guard, brought into Boston, and soon sold for Sea Scout training.  She was sold to British owners in 1930 and was registered at Bridgetown, Barbados, in 1936.  She was sunk by the Germans southeast of Trinidad on July 14, 1943.  The masts on these schooners were periodically scraped and then slushed down with a greasy mixture of various favorite ingredients.  We can guess from the pattern of chafe left by the masthoops that the *Harvard* is due for this treatment.

PLATE 41.  The *Yosemite* at anchor.  She was built by A. D. Story at Essex, Massachusetts, in 1891 for F. L. Davis, Captain John McFarland, and Captain William T. Lee of Gloucester.  Under the command of Captain John McKinnon while bound to Gloucester with a cargo of herring, she was wrecked off Ram Island, near Lockeport, Nova Scotia, on January 21, 1897.  The cook and one other in the crew were drowned.  The book, *Masts of Gloucester*, by Raymond McFarland, gives a colorful account of a voyage in this schooner.

PLATE 42. *(below)*. Schooners anchored in Brenton Cove. In *Masts of Gloucester*, Raymond McFarland speaks of entering Newport after two rough spring months hunting mackerel off the Virginia Capes, and of the joy of drying out and seeing green grass and trees again. Maybe this is the way the two men on the forestaysail boom feel. The coaster's mainsail advertises, "Quaker Ranges Win the Race."

PLATE 43. *(opposite)*. Beating in the East Passage in company with six other schooners. She has just been tacked and the Skipper is having a look up to windward.

PLATE 44. The *Speculator* running in, with Beavertail in the background. She was built by John James at Essex in 1895 for the Hugh Parkhurst Company in Gloucester. Her tonnage was 110 gross, 77 net. She was 96.2 feet long, 24.5 feet in beam, with a depth of 9.8 feet. She was sold to Saba, Dutch West Indies, in November, 1913, for trading.

PLATE 45.   The *Speculator* slides on by.  She has a bonnet on the jib.  Note the shadow of the main on the wung-out foresail.  Note also how the main topping lift is set up to take some of the weight of the boom off the sail.

PLATE 46. *(opposite)*. The New York Pilot schooner *Washington* visiting Newport. She was built at Brooklyn in 1884. Her tonnage was 70 gross, 66 net. She was 79.5 feet long, with a beam of 21.5 feet, and a depth of 8.9 feet. These vessels would sometimes come far to the eastward competing for business and then put into Narragansett Bay if they couldn't get back to New York in a northwest gale. Her big sail plan could be shortened down to almost nothing; note the double bonnets on forestaysail and jib and the depth and number of her reefs. She has a big yawl boat on deck, and her light boards are in the main rigging, instead of forward. The cylinder on the spring stay "turns off" and protects her lighted pilot boat lantern until she needs to show it.

PLATE 47. A towline helps bring this schooner in. Note how the seine boat has run up on her own tow line.

PLATE 48. A seiner drifting out by The Dumplings. She has a swordfishing pulpit rigged and a big jib topsail set. When making short tacks, the fisherman staysail would be left standing, so that on one tack — as shown here — the sail lay against the springstay and freshwater stay.

PLATE 49. *(opposite).* The *Norumbega* working up through the East Passage. She was built by Moses Adams at Essex in 1890 and was owned by Cunningham and Thompson of Gloucester. In 1895, G. A. McKenna was listed as her owner and master. Her net tonnage was 126.84. She was 107.5 feet long, with a beam of 24 feet, and a depth of 10.5 feet. She collided with the four-masted schooner, *Edith L. Allen,* off Fenwick Island on April 25, 1906 and was lost. She is about to tack off Hammersmith Farm; the helmsman looks astern, perhaps to see if he is clear of the photographer's catboat.

# PART II

## Coasting Schooners

Offshore we went, topmasts and flying jibboom bending to the pull of the sails and the loose gear flying in bights. Sant Lloyd at the wheel nursed the *Eugenie* carefully up across the steep crested seas, taking advantage of every little puff that let the schooner steal a few feet to windward and holding her to it when she shouldered into a curling sea that exploded into showers of spray leaping high above the weather bow. A mounting wave hissed along her lee quarter, some of it tumbling inboard and the rest breaking into froth as it merged with the wake astern.

— from John F. Leavitt's *Wake of the Coasters*

PLATE 50. The *Elbridge Gerry* heading out. She was built at Danversport, Massachusetts, in 1857 and was a Rockland lime coaster in the 1890s. Her tonnage was 71. There is considerable evidence of the different standard of seamanship practiced in the coasters, with their small crews, than on the fishermen, with their big gangs. The port anchor is still to be catted, one block of the yawlboat's fall is in the water, and the jib is loose with some of its gear trailing overboard.

*Preceding page.* Coasters drying out in the lower harbor. Fort Adams is in the background at the right.

PLATE 51. The *Island Belle* lying in Newport with the *Annie Pitcher* astern. The *Island Belle* was a Block Island boat, a local type of seaworthy double-ender developed at Block Island, twenty miles south and west of Newport, for fishing and general carrying. The *Island Belle* was Block Island's mail boat for years, making the run from Newport year round.

PLATE 52.   An unusual sloop-rigged coaster beating out against a light air from the south.  The schooner rig was far more popular, even for the smallest coasters, because of its greater variety of sail combinations and more easily handled mainsail.  The Captain has his umbrella set against the sun; the crew has the mainsail for shade.

PLATE 53. *(opposite).* Anchored in Newport Harbor. This vessel hails from Port Jefferson, Long Island. She is slightly hogged at the main rigging and has a double forestay. She could have brought a cargo of potatoes or sand or Long Island ducks to Narragansett Bay.

PLATE 54. The *Freestone* running in by Brenton Reef Lightship. She was built at Portland, Connecticut, in 1850 and hailed from Hartford, Connecticut. Her gross tonnage was 71. She was 73 feet long, with a beam of 25 feet, and a depth of 6.8 feet. She was one of a large fleet built on the Connecticut River to carry brownstone from the Portland Point quarries opposite Middletown to New York City. Note the fall hanging ready to pick up the yawl boat. She has no main topsail bent; the sail would help her considerably, but she is probably shorthanded.

PLATE 55.  The *Lyra* of St. John, New Brunswick, rides up over a swell as she puts to sea with a light, fair breeze.  She was built at Cambridge, New Brunswick, in 1883.  Her owner was Vincent S. White, and her master's name was Leonard.  Her gross tonnage was 99.  She was 83.1 feet long, with a beam of 27.3 feet, an a depth of 7 feet.  Note the slack in the port main topmast shrouds as the vessel rolls to weather.  Schooner rigging was generally not set up very hard.

PLATE 56. The *Sarah Jane* running in, with the Brenton Reef Light vessel well astern. She was built at Guilford, Connecticut, in 1848. Her gross tonnage was 74. Loaded deep and with a light breeze, she makes stately progress. But the steersman is right in style with his umbrella, and port is near. There is a yawl boat towing close under the stern.

PLATE 57. The *Stony Brook* of Port Jefferson ready to get up her anchor in Brenton Cove. She was built at Stony Brook, New York, in 1861. Her tonnage was 101.12 gross, 96.17 net. Note the number of blocks visible aloft. These are jig tackles on the standing ends of halyards and were used to sweat up the last few feet when making sail. She could be handled by the traditional "two men and a boy."

PLATE 58. The *Stony Brook*'s anchor is at the hawse and she has bare steerage way in the light air. It was plenty of work for two men to get underway in one of these little coasters with their heavy gear.

PLATE 59. Four coasters getting underway at Vineyard Haven after having been holed up waiting for a fair wind. The closest schooner is the *Thistle*, and the vessel anchored ahead of her is the *Cora May*. Both hailed from St. John, New Brunswick. The *Thistle* was built at Quaco, New Brunswick, was owned by Peter McIntyre, and was commanded by M. Hunter. Her gross tonnage was 123. She was 92.6 feet long, with a beam of 27.6 feet, and a depth of 7.9 feet. The *Cora May* was built at Black River, New Brunswick, in 1889. Her owner was N. C. Scott, and her master was Captain F. R. Fowler. Her gross tonnage was 125. She was 93 feet long, with a beam of 27.9 feet, and a depth of 7.4 feet. These vessels are homeward bound to the Maritime Provinces with coal from New York. Their outward cargoes would have been lumber, laths, or spruce piling.

PLATE 60.  "Coaster very heavy," commented the photographer on this vessel running in past Fort Dumpling. She appears to be a New York "canaler," perhaps carrying building stone. The structure amidships is called a "caboose." This house, which served as the galley, was lashed to ringbolts and could be moved away from the hatch to facilitate loading and discharge of cargo. Note the boom tackles rigged on both booms and the "bowline" on the leech of the forestaysail.

PLATE 61. Standing in past Castle Hill in a light easterly. A heavily laden vessel like this could keep going pretty well in a dying breeze. The main gaff has been fished.

PLATE 62. *(right)*. The *Cheehegen* reaching in on a quiet breeze. She was built in Montville, Connecticut in 1893. Her gross tonnage was 37.68, net 35.8. She was 54 feet long, with a beam of 21 feet, and a depth of 5.6 feet. This schooner maintained a regular freight service from Newport to Block Island in the Nineties. She looks to have a deck load of barrels of fish on this trip.

PLATE 63. *(below)*. Working up toward Coasters Harbor Island in light air. Note the downhauls on both gaffs and the running foretopmast backstay made up on the quarter. The ship is a training vessel at the Naval Station. Gull Rocks Light appears under the end of the main boom.

PLATE 64. The *Ervin J. Luce* running in past Castle Hill. She was built at New London in 1892. Her tonnage was 127.45 gross, 121.08 net. In later years she was owned by the Rockport Granite Company, Rockport, Massachusetts. The first reef band in the foresail seems to have been recently reinforced.

PLATE 65. Waiting for a breeze off The Dumplings. A morning northerly has died, and she is becalmed at noonday, waiting for the afternoon sou'wester to make up. Whether the tide is carrying her out to meet the breeze or back up the Bay would govern the Skipper's mood. The vessel steaming out is the U.S.S. *Dolphin*, one of the famous ABCD ships (the *Atlanta, Boston, Chicago,* and *Dolphin*), the Navy's first steel warships. She was used to deliver orders prior to the introduction of radio.

PLATE 66.   Beating out light. Beavertail Light is just visible astern and the West
Passage is on the lee quarter. Her sails are flattened in nicely, and she seems
to be footing well, some six points off the wind.

PLATE 67. *(below).* Running in wing-and-wing. She is sailing with the mainsail by the lee to keep the foresail and its topsail from jibing. Probably the main was put over a little after this picture was taken, as she passed The Dumplings and went on up the Bay on the port tack.

PLATE 68. *(opposite).* The *Sally W. Ponder* and four other coasters making the best of a dying northwest breeze. The Dumplings are on her weather quarter and Rose Island is astern. She was built in 1855 at Milford, Delaware. Her tonnage was 107 gross, 102 net. She was 86.6 feet long, with a beam of 25.4 feet, and a depth of 6.4 feet. She looks to be in good shape for such an elderly vessel.

PLATE 69. A "riz-deck" lime carrier from Rockland, Maine, boiling along
full-and-by. Her long poop stopped just abaft the foremast; its purpose was
to increase the capacity of the vessel to carry lime below decks. Many schooners
did carry lime casks on deck, but it was a dangerous practice. With booms
lifting and topmasts straining, she carries her heavy cargo at a good speed. The
coasters had much longer and higher jibbooms than the fishermen. With their
smaller crews, they used the fore topsail, rather than the fisherman staysail.
She has a lift rigged to the clew of her boomless jib. What are the two men
on the fore hatch yarning about?

PLATE 70. Carrying a deck load of sawn lumber in past Brenton Reef Lightship. Note the topsails, one to windward and one to leeward of the peak halyards, so that one would set to advantage on each tack. She has a preventer rigged to hold the main boom out.

PLATE 71. *(below)*. Reaching in on a southeaster. The pull of the big jib topsail puts a sag in its stay. Soon her crew will be busy working her up to an anchorage in the harbor and getting the sail off her. Her full-length box rail shows she has a long "riz" deck.

PLATE 72. *(opposite)*. Loaded deep and coming in across a flat summer sea. She has an unusually short jibboom and lazy jacks rigged on the jib, Chesapeake Bay style. When the sail was dropped the lazy jacks gathered it on the boom so the crew could forget about it until they were ready to furl up.

PLATE 73. The *Altana M. Jagger* of Providence standing in past Castle Hill. She was built at Wilmington, Delaware, in 1890. Her tonnage was 132 gross, 125 net. She was 102.4 feet long, 22 feet in beam, with a depth of 7.8 feet. Her flowing sheer with high shoulders forward and a tucked-up stern show her to be a fine example of the able, burdensome coasting schooner. She was one of the last schooners to work on Long Island Sound.

PLATE 74. The *Ina* of St. John, standing along shore under full sail. She was built at Waterboro, New Brunswick, in 1890, and was owned and sailed by Captain L. S. Hanselpacker. She is descended from the "Johnny woodboats," built principally for carrying cord and kiln wood. Her distinguishing features are the high stern, high house aft, and an outboard rudder. The original Johnny woodboats were bald-headed and had no headsails, with the foremast stepped way forward in the eyes. They, in turn, were direct descendants of the Colonial shallops and Chebacco boats.

PLATE 75. The *Valdare*, of St. John, New Brunswick, another latter-day Johnny woodboat, easing out. She was built by J. S. Robinson at Cambridge, New Brunswick, in 1888. She was owned by Peter McIntyre and commanded by a Leonard, possibly the same man who had been master of the *Lyra*. Her gross tonnage was 100. She was 83 feet long, with a beam of 27 feet, and a depth of 7.2 feet. The peak halyard on the foresail has been slacked off, and the boom allowed to droop, perhaps to try to make the sail draw better in the light breeze. Note the shallow "lumber reefs" on the foresail and mainsail, used to keep the booms clear of a deck load.

PLATE 76. The *Manson* of New Bedford, a hermaphrodite brig, running down the Bay. She was built at Brewer, Maine, in 1867. Her tonnage was 264.36 gross, 231.15 net. She was 105.2 feet long, with a beam of 26.5 feet and a depth of 12.4 feet. While coastwise cargo vessels were generally fore-and-aft rigged and deepwater freighters were usually square-rigged, circumstances often dictated that a sizeable coaster would sail foreign or that a small square-rigger like this one would follow a coastal route. The *Manson* was built to go foreign but ended up in the coastwise trade.

PLATE 77. The *Manson* runs on by. The top of her main topmast was probably carried away in a gale. Note the double tackles on the main boom, one to each quarter, and the deep reefs in the mainsail. Her light boards are aft in the main rigging. Her rig is noticeably complex compared to a schooner; her modest crew has been busy to make so much sail while still in the Bay. The boat on the forward house is the famous 19-foot whaleboat *New Bedford*, in which the *Manson*'s master, Captain Thomas Crapo, sailed across the Atlantic with his wife in the summer of 1877. The voyage from Chatham, at the elbow of Cape Cod, to Newlyn, England, took 49 days. Captain Crapo bought the *Manson* in 1895. She carried lumber and general merchandise between Boston, Philadelphia, and Norfolk. Mrs. Crapo often sailed in the *Manson* and was considered a fit first officer. Captain Crapo lost the *Manson* — and with her the *New Bedford*, stowed on board as usual—on January 9, 1898 when she got ashore near Delaware breakwater in thick fog. Captain Crapo himself was lost in May, 1899, attempting to sail from Newport to Cuba in a nine-foot boat named the *Volunteer*.

PLATE 78. The *Starlight* drifting in from sea. She was built at East Haven, Connecticut, in 1874. Her tonnage was 256 gross, 216 net. She was 116 feet long, with a beam of 29 feet, and a depth of 11 feet. Note that her upper topsail would be quite small when reefed. This made a good heavy weather sail, for, unlike a schooner's foresail, it was high enough to escape alternate collapsing and then filling with a bang as the vessel first fell into the trough and then climbed the next sea.

PLATE 79. The *Starlight* has taken a rower in tow. Note how her topmasts and topgallant mast are sprung well forward.

PLATE 80. *(opposite).* The *Stacy Clark* of Boston running up the Bay. She was built at Waldoboro, Maine, in 1879, the last hermaphrodite brig built there. Her gross tonnage was 352.2. She was 136 feet long, with a beam of 30.2 feet, and a depth of 12 feet. She foundered off Cape Hatteras on October 24, 1897. Perhaps it is her Skipper in the white shirt, peering over the deck load he is bringing in, probably logwood from the West Indies.

PLATE 81. The *Stacy Clark* braced up on a light breeze. Her cargo has been discharged, and she is outward bound. Her royal yard has been sent aloft. Note the weather foresheet draped over the boat skid.

PLATE 82.   The *Abel W. Parker* of Nantucket standing in.  She was built at Boothbay, Maine, in 1873.  She was registered in Chesapeake Bay as late as the Thirties.  Her tonnage was 202.76 gross, 192.36 net.  She was 116.1 feet long, with a beam of 32.2 feet, and a depth of 7.9 feet.  Note the port bower at the cathead.  Its stock seems to be bent, which was not uncommon or surprising, considering the heavy use a coaster made of her anchors.  The flying jib has been hauled down, and perhaps the hand by the fore rigging will presently lay out on the jibboom to tie it up.

PLATE 83.   The *Douglas Haynes* of Bath stomping up the Bay with a big deck-load of lumber.  She was built at Bath, Maine, in 1872.  Her tonnage was 173 gross, 165 net.  She was 104.2 feet long, 28.4 feet in beam, with a depth of 7.7 feet.  Note that though she is trimmed in tight, her fore gaff sags far off to leeward.  This was common with sails having boom and gaff nearly the same length.

PLATE 84. *(right).* The *Lizzie Lane* running in. She was built at Searsport, Maine, in 1874. Her tonnage was 231 gross, 219 net. She was 115.8 feet long, with a beam of 29.8 feet, and a depth of 9.2 feet. Her Skipper has had to climb up on the high deck load so he can see where his vessel is going and give orders to the helmsman. The vessel has just been jibed over and the mizzen springstay and mizzen topmast stay have kept the main topsail and mainsail from swinging across.

PLATE 85. *(below).* The *Benjamin T. Biggs* of New York running in wing-and-wing. She was built at Milton, Delaware, in 1870. Her tonnage was 163.96 gross, 155.76 net. Her main topsail is clewed up to the mast and its sheet is visible running through its block on the end of the gaff. She has new clews worked into her jibs. Her deck cargo is lumber.

PLATE 86. The big three-master, *Morris W. Child* of Boston, standing in close-hauled in a light northwester with a deckload of lumber. She was built at Camden, Maine, in 1881. Her tonnage was 512.86 gross, 487.22 net. She was 144 feet long, with a beam of 34 feet, and a depth of 12.25 feet. Note the coiled jib gaskets hanging from the jibboom. She was beached at the entrance to Cardenas, Cuba, on January 6, 1902 after striking a rock. Her cargo of coal was partly salvaged.

PLATE 87. *(below).* The *Abbie Bowker* of Bath picking up a new southwest breeze off Castle Hill. She was built at Phippsburg, Maine, in 1890. Her tonnage was 191.72 gross, 182.14 net. She was 104.7 feet long, 29.6 feet in beam, with a depth of 8.6 feet. The foretopsail sheet has been slacked and soon the sail will be shifted over the stays, the flying jib set, the anchor fished up to the rail, the yawl brought up to the davit heads, and then she'll be on her way, beating out in the rising breeze.

PLATE 88. *(opposite).* Running in all wung out to a moderate southwest breeze. This view shows off the handsome sheer and tumble home of this schooner's hull. A triangular main topmast staysail is just visible, visually coinciding almost exactly with the upper part of the main topsail.

PLATE 89. The *Jennie C. May* of Norwalk, Connecticut, standing down the East Passage in ballast. Captain Oscar St. John was her managing owner and master. She was built at Bath, Maine, in 1889. Her tonnage was 882 gross, 745 net. She was 177.8 feet long, with a beam of 35.8 feet, and a depth of 16.7 feet. She was lost in 1902. A leading breeze was all-important with the vessel so high out of water she could scarcely work to windward. Many of the coasters had center-boards, which were particularly helpful when the schooner was light. The dead-eyes and lanyards used to set up the rigging show clearly; they required frequent attention as the rigging worked and stretched. Two men observe the scene from the weather quarter.

PLATE 90.   The *Jennie C. May* sails by, weathering Beavertail nicely.  The handsome yawl boat's slack painter makes a graceful curve at the stern.  The vertical patch in the jib may tell of a flogging that was too much for the sail, perhaps when it was being taken in during a squall.

PLATE 91. *(below)*.    The *Joseph G. Dean* of New Bedford coasting along in a light
air.  She was built at Kennebunk, Maine, in 1882.  Her tonnage was 161.73 gross,
153.65 net.  She was a shoal-draft centerboarder with a reputation as a very smart
sailer.  Note the "caboose" forward of the mainmast.  She looks a most handsome
schooner, with her long bowsprit and jibboom, her graceful sheer line, and her
nicely setting sails.

PLATE 92. *(opposite)*.    The *William O. Snow* of Taunton taking in sail as she eases
into port.  She was built in 1881 at Bath, Maine, by Goss and Sawyer for J. H.
Rhodes and other owners from Taunton, Massachusetts.  Her first managing
owner was Samuel H. Walker of Taunton.  Her tonnage was 560.  She was 153
feet long, with a beam of 35 feet, and a depth of 15 feet.  Her flying jib has been
hauled down and the foretopsail sheet has been slacked in readiness to clew up the
sail.  The sail visible under the mizzen boom belongs to another schooner that may
be overtaking this big brute.

PLATE 93.  The *Marguerite* of Fall River running in with all her laundry hung out. She was built at Bath, Maine, in 1889.  Her three topmast staysails aren't doing much before the wind, but on a reach in light weather they were well worth setting.  She certainly had plenty of jibs.  It took time to handle the sheets when she was put about.  Note the windsail set just forward of the mainmast to funnel air into the galley in the midship house.

PLATE 94.   The *Maud B. Krum* standing in.  She was built in 1883 at Bath, Maine, as the three-masted bark, *Amy*.  Her tonnage was 700.15 gross, 665.15 net.  She was 159.1 feet long, 35.5 feet in beam, with a depth of 16.7 feet.  In 1905, she was re-rigged and renamed.  She went missing in 1915 bound from St. Andrews, Florida, to Buenos Aires.  Note the fancy wind indicator at the spanker truck.  It was coal barges like those astern, being towed by a tug behind the vessel, that brought an end to coasting schooners.

PLATE 95.  The *Clara E. McGilvery* of Searsport running in.  She was built at
Searsport, Maine, in 1873 by J. B. Dunbar.  Her tonnage was 402 gross, 332 net.
She was 126.6 feet long, with a beam of 30.3 feet, and a depth of 11.4 feet.  At one
time she was commanded by Captain Lincoln Colcord, who sailed with his wife
and two children, Lincoln, Jr., and Joanna, both later well-known maritime histor-
ians.  She was sold to Nova Scotia in 1898 and was abandoned off the Carolina
coast the next year while owned by John Nutt of Port Medway, Nova Scotia.
She is clearly a deep-sea vessel, with her sharply steeved bowsprit, raked masts,
and curved transom.  Note that her light boards are aft in the mizzen rigging.

PLATE 96. The *Clara E. McGilvery* eases by with her deckload of lumber. These views show an advantage of the barkentine rig over the schooner: running before it, the sails on the foremast are full, instead of being blanketed by the after sails. It is interesting that the barkentine rig survived as long as did the schooner and was in use up to the time of World War II on the West Coast. The foresail sheet, leading through a fairlead in the side, shows how deep were her bulwarks, while the men standing aft by the rail indicate the height of her quarterdeck. Note the ladder stowed across the stern davits.

PLATE 97. The *Thomas Brown* steaming down the Bay. She represents an advanced modern tugboat of the Nineties. She was stationed in Fall River and occasionally used to come down to Newport to pick up a schooner that had been becalmed or abnormally delayed by adverse weather. From the fountain at her bow, pushed up by her broad stem moving through the water, right up to the giant rooster atop her wheelhouse, she shows herself to be a vessel of real character. One can be sympathetic with the pride of her master, who can just be made out in the wheelhouse, wearing a white shirt, tie, and vest.

PLATE 98.  Brenton Reef Lightship No. 11 on station.  She was anchored off Brenton Reef about two miles from shore and was a point of entry and departure for schooners entering and leaving Narragansett Bay.  At the time this picture was taken, at the end of her service, she came to national attention in a magazine article about a sea gull named "Dick."  Dick was taught by the lightship crew to get food at a regular hour from the vessel.  The success of their lessons was evident by the fact that the bird visited the ship every day from the 1st of October to the 1st of April over a period of twenty-four years.  The story captured the imagination of the country.

PLATE 99.   The *Gov. Ames* working out by Fort Adams.   The first five-masted schooner built, she was launched at Waldoboro, Maine, in 1888.   Her tonnage was 1,778 gross, 1,597 net.   She was 245.6 feet long, with a beam of 49.6 feet, and a depth of 21.2 feet.   Once she rounded Cape Horn, picked up a cargo of lumber on the West Coast, and took it to the South Seas.   Returning round the Horn, she struck rough weather, and her Master opined that this sort of vessel should never again be used for deep-water passages.   Her experimental voyage was not successful.   (See text, page 165.)  When she tacked, her four forward topsails and her four topmast staysails had to be shifted over.   She was lost in 1910.

PLATE 100.  The *William C. Carnegie* of Portland close-hauled under full sail. She was built at Bath, Maine, by Percy and Small in 1900 and was owned by J. S. Winslow and Company.  Her tonnage was 2,664 gross, 2,381 net.  She was 289.2 feet long, with a beam of 46.3 feet, and a depth of 22.4 feet.  Here is a fine example of the big, handsome coasting schooner under a cloud of canvas moving a large cargo using only the free power of the wind.

PLATE 101. *(below).* The *Mary F. Barrett* of Bath wung out with the boom tackles rigged. She was built at Bath, Maine, by G. G. Deering in 1901. Her tonnage was 1,833 gross, 1,563 net. She was 241.3 feet long, 43.3 feet in beam, with a depth of 24.6 feet. Her mizzen, spanker, and jigger are catching what little breeze there is.

PLATE 102. *(opposite).* The *Mary F. Barrett* runs on by. She has been slowed down by lack of wind, and there is not much hope of improved conditions, judging by the steamer's smoke ahead. The *Barrett's* bones are still visible at Robin Hood Cove, below Bath, where she was laid up to die.

# 1 / The Gloucester Fishing Schooner

## HOWARD I. CHAPELLE

THE GLOUCESTER FISHING SCHOONERS NEED NO INTRODUCTION TO yachtsmen. Fast, seaworthy and handsome, they have long been admired by all seamen. The early types are of particular interest as they influenced the design of many other classes of schooners in America.

The development of the fast sailing Gloucester schooner may be said to have started with the building of the little *Romp*. The advantages of speed in a fishing schooner were first appreciated by the Essex modeler and builder, Andrew Story, who, in order to demonstrate these advantages to the conservative fishermen, built a small schooner on speculation during the winter of 1846-47. This vessel was the famous *Romp*. Taking the then well-known Baltimore clipper schooner as a model, Andrew Story turned out a vessel that retained most of the speed of the fast southern schooners, but with added capacity, seaworthiness and dryness. The new schooner had the low freeboard, deep drag to the keel, raking ends, straight sheer, and marked deadrise of the Baltimore flyers, combined with harder bilges and longer body, to give cargo capacity. Her bow, too, differed from that of a typical Baltimore schooner in that it was very round and full on deck, but due to the great flare employed was rather sharp on the water line.

So wedded to the old types were the fishermen that it was some time before Story could sell his vessel. At last a man who had lost his old vessel was

Reprinted from *American Sailing Craft* by Howard I. Chapelle, by permission of the author. This section was Chapters V and VI of the above book, published by Kennedy Brothers, New York, in 1936.

113

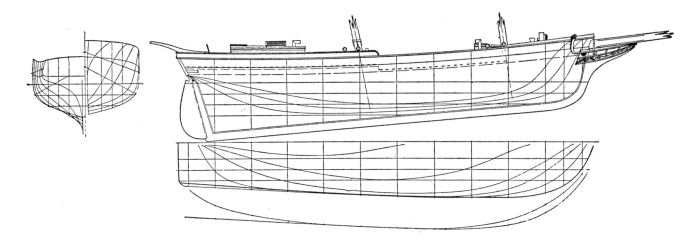

FIGURE 1.   *Lines of a sharpshooter Grand Banker of 1850. Length over-all, 68 feet, 6 inches; registered length, 65 feet, 5 inches; extreme beam, 18 feet; and depth of hold, 6 feet. Built at Essex, Massachusetts.*

prevailed upon to purchase the new schooner.  When it came time to fit out, great difficulty was found in getting men to sail on her, as she was considered too sharp for safety.  At last a crew was procured and the *Romp* got to sea, not without many misgivings on the part of the waterfront "experts."  By the time the *Romp* had reached the fishing banks her reputation was established; not only had she proved her seaworthiness and speed to her own doubting crew, but to those of all vessels she had met.

Her success established by her first trip, copies of the new schooner were at once built.  Because of the great deadrise usually employed, vessels of the new type were soon nicknamed "file-bottoms," and, later, "sharp-shooters."  After a long career as a fisherman, the *Romp* carried a party of gold-seekers around Cape Horn to California.  From 1849 to 1857, the sharp-shooter was the popular type of fisherman, but during the late Fifties the model underwent a rapid change.

From builders' half-models, sailmakers' plans, pictures, and a few rigged models that are contemporary, it is possible to show just what the sharpshooter looked like.  In Figure 1 will be seen the lines of a sharpshooter built at Essex in

114

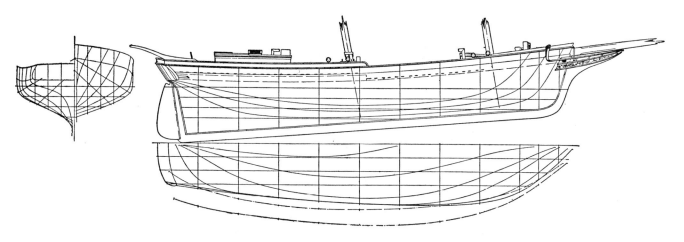

FIGURE 2. *A sharpshooter market fisherman built in 1853. Length over-all, 62 feet, 6 inches; registered length, 58 feet, 6 inches; extreme beam, 18 feet; and depth of hold, 5 feet, 3 inches. Built at Essex, Massachusetts.*

1850, for Beverly owners. The bankers, because they stayed out on the banks until they had a full cargo of fish, or "fare," salted down, were more of the carrier type than were the market boats, which made rapid trips to the inshore banks and brought home fresh fish in wet wells, or iced. The banker in Figure 1, it will be noticed, was quite burdensome for her length. The full, round, and sharply flaring bow shown was known at Essex as the "cartwheel bow," and was considered necessary to prevent the vessel from diving when at anchor on the banks in heavy weather.

To illustrate the difference between the banker and the market boat, the lines of a sharpshooter market schooner are shown in Figure 2. This vessel was built at Essex about 1853, and is, for her time, an extremely sharp schooner. It will be noticed that her displacement is relatively less than that of the banker, and that she is much sharper. The necessity of speed was greater in the case of the market boats than in that of the bankers, as fresh fish do not long remain in good condition.

The heads of the sharpshooters were long and had a pointed look; the

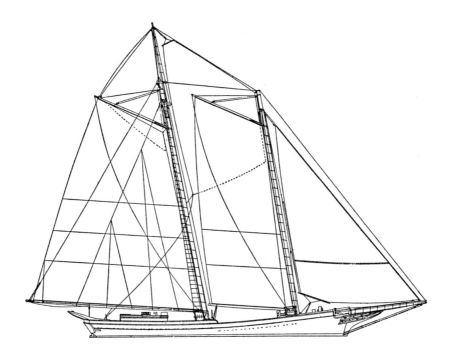

FIGURE 3. *Sail plan of the sharpshooter shown on page 115.*

bowsprit had little steeve, often being "hogged" down, as in the Chesapeake skipjacks or bugeyes of more recent times. The heads were supported by a single headrail on each side, and by cheek knees and carved trail boards, finishing off forward with a simple billet or fiddle-head. The sterns had very little overhang. The early sharpshooters had the old-fashioned transom, the lower portion of which was set at a more acute angle than the upper, and the rudder stock went up through the lower transom face rather than through the counter, as was almost universally the case after 1850. The top of the transom was square-cornered, but as the mainsheet had a tendency to catch these corners, the elliptical transom seen on modern schooners was introduced in the beautiful little sharpshooter *Ripple,* built at Essex in 1853 by Joseph Story. One of the first schooners to have the long overhang counter was the *Break O' Day,* put up in 1859, but a number of years passed before this type of stern became general in the fishing fleet.

The sharpshooters were built of oak throughout, except for the decks, which were of white pine. The planking was between two and three inches thick up to the level of the quarter deck plank-sheer, and a three-inch band of white was painted along this plank-sheer and carried forward to the stem. Above, there were a couple of strakes of thin planking, an inch or so in thickness, extending to the rail cap. The line formed by the two thicknesses of planking is the waist, and up to the late Sixties, the waist in the sharpshooters was at the quarter deck planksheer level. Later it was a few inches above the quarter deck scuppers. The topsides were painted black or dark green, the underbody green or copper color and the decks and fittings gray or white. Sometimes there was a multi-colored stripe above the planksheer and below the "waist."

Figure 3 represents the sail and deck plans of the schooner shown in Figure 2. The rig was simple, differing but little from the then popular pilot boat rig. The masts had a strong rake and there was a bonnet in the jib. The only difference between the rig of the bankers and that shown was that the former was relatively smaller and a maintopsail was rarely carried, though sometimes a dummy maintopmast was rigged. The deck plan was almost standardized until comparatively recent years. Beginning forward, there was a pump brake windlass (the handspike windlass was used in the Forties), abaft this was the wooden jib sheet horse extending from bulwark to bulwark, supported by bulwark stanchions, which also supported cavil cleats. This horse was five or six inches in diameter, square at the ends, and some five inches above the deck. At each end, about eighteen inches inboard of the bulwarks, a bolt was driven, with its head flush, and extending about three inches below the horse. These bolts acted as stops for the traveler, which was a plain iron ring. Then came the foremast, with either a wooden collar for belaying pins, or a fife rail. The

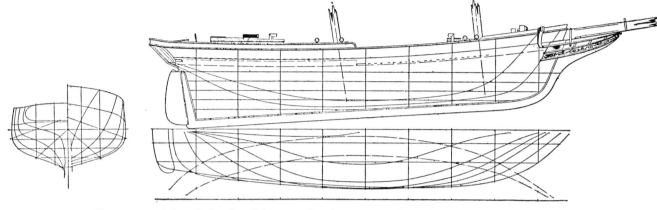

FIGURE 4.   *The salt banker fisherman,* Lookout, *1857. Length over-all, 68 feet, 3 inches; registered length, 62 feet, 10 inches; extreme beam, 19 feet, 6 inches; and depth of hold, 6 feet. Modelled by Charles O. Story. Twenty or more schooners, among them the* Laughing Water, Fish Hawk, Arizona, *and* E. K. Kane, *were built from this model at Essex, Massachusetts, between 1858 and 1865.*

forecastle companionway was close abaft the foremast, and was combined with a small hatch to the hold. The two openings had a common coaming, about 4'-8" long and 36 inches wide, and were separated by a beam under which was a bulkhead. The forward of the two openings was covered by a slide and companionway, which overhung the coaming forward almost to the mast. This was the entrance to the forecastle. The after opening was covered by an ordinary hatch cover and a portable grating. Amidships was the main hatch, about 4'-6" square, and abaft this the "great beam," or break in the deck, the rise to the quarter deck being from eight to ten inches.

On the quarter deck was the foresheet horse, of iron, and the main mast, with its fife rail, came next. Just abaft the mainmast and under the fife rail were two wooden pumps, bored out of solid logs, eight or nine inches in outside diameter, extending up about 26 inches, to the underside of the fife rails, through which holes were bored to enable the pump plungers to be lifted out. The plungers were operated by levers pivoted on iron brackets shaped somewhat like oarlocks, the shanks of which extended through the fife rail and also the deck.

Abaft the pumps was another hatch, 4 feet long and 4'-6" wide. Then came a large grating laid on deck just forward of the cabin trunk. Sometimes a deck box replaced the after portion of the grating. The cabin trunk had no ports. There was a slide and a skylight on the roof, and also the stack of the cabin stove. Many schooners had a long "barrel head box" on the fore end of the trunk. Abaft the trunk was the wheelbox (tillers were used in the Forties), and the quarter bitts. The main sheet horse, of iron, was on the "seat" over the transom, but sometimes quarter blocks were used. Wooden stern davits were used to carry a boat.

From 1855 to 1860 there was a period of experimentation, the desire for speed in the fishing schooners having become almost a mania. However, there were some conservative models still built. Figure 4 shows one of these, a banker. On these lines, the *Lookout* was built, in 1857, at Essex. Designed by Charles O. Story and built in the yard of Joseph Story, the *Lookout* was a popular vessel for use on the Grand Banks and the Georges. So well was she liked that some twenty other schooners were built on her molds during the next ten years. Though a good carrier, the *Lookout* was much sharper than the banker of the Fifties. Even in this class of vessel there was a marked decrease in depth.

It was in the market fleet that the more extreme schooners were developed. During the late Fifties, each new market schooner was shoaler, wider, and sharper-ended than the last, until the new "clippers" came into existence about 1857. Heralded by two extreme schooners modeled by Charles O. Story, the *Etta G. Fogg* and the *George Fogg,* built at Essex in that year, the clippers soon replaced the older type. The two mentioned were built for Wellfleet owners and were employed in the market fishery in the summer and in the Chesapeake Bay oyster trade during the winter. They were shoal, keel vessels, in order to enter the southern oyster ports, and were very fast. The success of these and similar schooners soon led to vessels of even more extreme type.

Such a schooner is shown in Figure 5, the *Flying Fish,* modeled and built by Jeremiah Burnham in 1860 at Essex, as a fast market schooner. Though considered an extreme vessel when built, she was a common type for the next 25 years. The *Flying Fish* was an extremely fast ship; in fact, for some years she was looked upon as being the fastest schooner in the fleet. After being employed as a fisherman for some time, she was sold to New London for use as a sealer and sea elephant hunter,

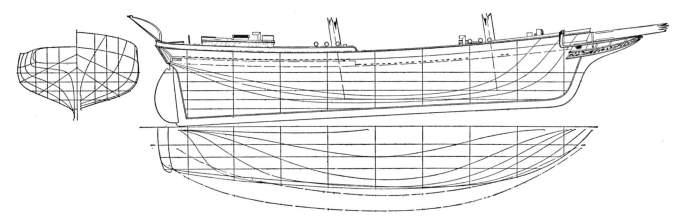

FIGURE 5. *The* Flying Fish, *1860, one of the first of the "clipper" models used in the fisheries. Length over-all, 74 feet; registered length, 70 feet, 6 inches; extreme beam, 21 feet; and depth of hold, 6 feet, 3 inches. Built at Essex, Massachusetts, by Jeremiah Burnham.*

though it would seem difficult to find a type more unsuited to the rigors of the weather off Cape Stiff than this high-hatted, Essex-built flyer.

The lines of the *Flying Fish* show the characteristics of the clipper type. Perhaps the most apparent of these were the shoalness of the hull and its very marked hollowness at bow and stern. Compared to the older sharpshooters, the clipper had little drag and lower bilges, combined with great proportionate beam. Practically all of this type had very raking midsections, remarkably long hollow runs, and, usually, rather heavy quarters. From all accounts, the clippers sailed best when nearly on even keel, probably because of the heavy lee quarter which was a drag when well heeled. When rolled down, rails under, they were apt to capsize or take a knockdown.

In appearance, the clipper was distinguished by her low freeboard, rather short counter, and the typical long, heavy head. Many of the heads seen on vessels of this class had one more headrail than is shown in the plan of the *Flying Fish*. This rail was above the long rail (to the underside of the cathead) was supported by iron rods to the rail below and reached from the billet to the foreside of the

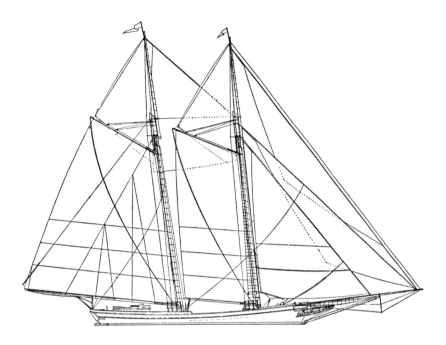

FIGURE 6. *Sail plan of the* Flying Fish.

catheads. Only the large vessels seem to have had this feature.

These vessels were painted very like the sharpshooters, and had the same white band along the quarter deck planksheer and forward; when the waist line was raised (some time in the late Sixties apparently), another stripe was added, of red, just above the quarter deck scuppers. Some time in the Seventies the practice of painting the bulwarks a dark bottle green, with the remaining portion of the hull black, became popular, and finally, it became fairly common to see hulls all green, the shade being either an olive or dark bottle green. Red copper paint became very popular in the Gloucester fleet soon after the Civil War.

As employed on the fishing schooner, the catheads were small, with but little spread. They were merely bolted to the bulwark stanchions after the planking had been put on. The long headrail widened as it approached and curved up to the underside of the cathead.

Figure 6 shows the deck and sail plan of the *Flying Fish*, the last being taken from the sailmaker's drawings. The deck arrangement varies but little from that seen in the sharpshooters, and requires no further comment. The height of some of the deck structures was as follows: samson post, 4 feet; windlass bitts, 3'6"; fife rails, 28 to 30 inches; companionway, 2'3" at after end, 20 inches at the fore, exclusive of a slide 3 inches high. The hatch coamings were from 12 to 14 inches high; the topsail bitts supporting the fore end of the main fife rail, 42 inches, or thereabouts. The cabin trunk was usually quite high in the clippers, varying from 30 to 36 inches in height above the quarter deck; the quarter bitts were 21 inches in height and sided about 8 inches.

The rig is worthy of attention, if for no other reason than its size. While the contemporary bankers, such as *Lookout*, carried a small edition of the same sail plan, they rarely had foretopmasts. The market schooners, however, had a complete rig, as shown. Only in winter were the topmasts and jibboom left at home. All standing rigging was of hemp, as in the sharpshooters, the jibstay being about three inches in diameter. The jibstay passed through the bowsprit and shackled into the stem, while the bobstay reached from the stem to a band on the bowsprit. Both were tarred and wrapped in canvas, with a rawhide cover, to a few feet above the water line. Chain was sometimes used for the lower bobstay. The jib hanks were of wood, as were the mast rings. The big jib had a bonnet, and this practice was carried well into the Eighties. In old photographs the jibboom is usually shown well "hogged" down. Because of the long boom and the position of the main sheet, breakage was very common and it was the custom to take along a number of timbers to "fish" the spar when an accident occurred. The jibboom was usually on the side of the bowsprit, to clear the jibstay.

In spite of the danger incurred in the use of this type, the clippers were widely copied because of their speed. It is also claimed, by old men who sailed in them, that when hove-to they were more comfortable than the more able modern schooners, having a tendency to slide to leeward on the face of a comber. At any

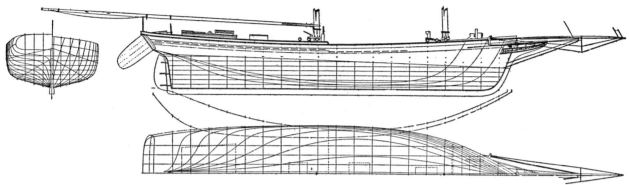

FIGURE 7. *The* Grace L. Fears, *built in 1874, typical of the trend in design between 1870 and 1880. Built by David Alfred Story at Gloucester. The* Bunker Hill *was also built to this model.*

rate, the coasters, West Indian fruiters, and the fishermen built in Maine and Nova Scotia, were copies of the Essex-built clippers. It took many years and a great loss of lives and vessels to convince fishermen that a better type was possible.

The trend of the design of Gloucester fishing schooners during the period between 1870 and the early 1880's was toward such extremes of the so-called "clipper" type as were apparent in the *Grace L. Fears*, Figure 7. This vessel had all the characteristics of her type—low, hard bilges, low bulwarks, shallow hold and a large rig. She was built at Gloucester by David Alfred Story in 1874. On the same molds other schooners were built during the next few years, among them the *Bunker Hill*. The *Fears* is best remembered as the schooner from which Howard Blackburn became separated, bringing about the death of his dory-mate and his long row to shore, the result of which was the loss of his hands and toes from freezing. Such vessels as the *Fears* were popular in all classes of the fisheries, even on the Grand Banks, during these years.

During the Eighties, Captain J. W. Collins, a Gloucester skipper, joined the United States Fish Commission and, conscious that much of the fearful loss of lives and vessels could be traced to the bad features of the type of schooner then in use, began to write on the necessity of a new class of vessel. The Gloucester news-papers carried this discussion in their columns and much argument resulted. The builders and modelers gave thought to the subject and, in 1884, the famous *Roulette* was launched at East Boston, by Dennison J. Lawlor. Lawlor was born in New Brunswick and started modeling and building at East Boston about 1850. Though he had built a number of fishing schooners, such as the *Sylph* in '65, the *Sarah H. Cressy* in '66, and the *Helen M. Foster* in '71, he was best known as the designer and builder of pilot boats. In the same year that he laid down the *Roulette* he built the great *Hesper*, long considered the fastest of all pilot schooners.

The *Roulette* was a sensation. Not only was she about two feet deeper in the hold and much sharper in the floors than any of her contemporaries, but she proved to be a very fast sailer and more weatherly than any schooner in the fleet. Though the *Roulette* was built for a Philadelphia firm, she usually worked out of Boston, and during the latter part of her existence was owned there.

While the *Roulette* was building at East Boston, the other builders and de-signers were not idle. Captain Collins had been on friendly terms with Lawlor and with his help had modeled a new schooner for the Fish Commission, which was laid down at Noank, Conn., and launched the next year (1885). At about the same time, Arthur D. Story began to build a schooner on pilot boat lines at Essex. The *Roulette* had a plumb stem but also had a gammon knee head, which did not im-prove her appearance. The pilot schooners had been given plumb and straight stems for many years, and the two new schooners followed this style. The Fish Commission's new schooner was named the *Grampus* and was quite successful. The Essex vessel, Figure 8, was launched about the same time as the *Grampus* and was named for her builder, *Arthur D. Story*. She was employed mostly as a banker, going to Iceland regularly for cod. Eventually she was lost with all hands. It is said that she and another schooner were driven under, side by side, while under a press of sail.

The plan of the *Arthur D. Story* may be taken as an example of the new class of fishing schooner. Unfortunately, I am unable to find out who modeled her; perhaps Lawlor should have credit for her, too. The new pilot boat model fishing schooners had the same rig as the older boats, the change was in lines and size. It may be interesting to compare the vessels already mentioned. The *Fears*

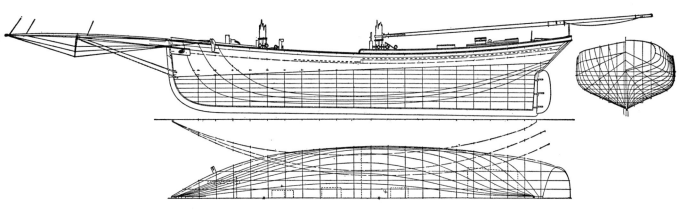

FIGURE 8. *The forerunner of the "plumb stemmers," the* Arthur D. Story, *1885. Built by Arthur D. Story at Essex, Massachusetts, for Benjamin Low of Gloucester.*

measured 84.50 tons net, 81 feet long, 22.9 feet beam and 10 feet depth of hold; the *Grampus* was 83.3 tons net, 81 feet long, 22.4 feet beam, and 10 feet depth of hold, and the *Story* was 98.61 tons net, 85 feet long, 23.3 feet beam and 9.6 feet depth of hold. These measurements, it should be noted, are for tonnage and are not strictly accurate; however, they give a measure of comparison. It will be seen that there was a great increase in carrying capacity in the new vessels in addition to a change of form. The pilot schooner model introduced a new type of stern, as will be seen in the plans of the *Story*, which was popular for a few years. The success of the vessels built in 1884 and 1885 resulted in a number of "plumb stemmers," such as the *Puritan*, in 1887, and the *J. H. Carey*, in 1888, all fine able schooners. However, a new vessel that was to mark the turning point in the Gloucester fleet had come out about this time.

In 1886, Benjamin Phillips, of Boston, commissioned the rising young yacht designer, Edward Burgess, to draw plans for a fast, big schooner and Arthur D. Story built her at Essex that winter. This was the well-known *Carrie E. Phillips*, Figure 9. She measured 109.99 tons net, was 93.5 feet long, 24. 9 feet beam, and 11 feet depth of hold. The *Phillips* was an innovation in more ways than one and she was even deeper and with more rising floors than the earlier schooners; she had

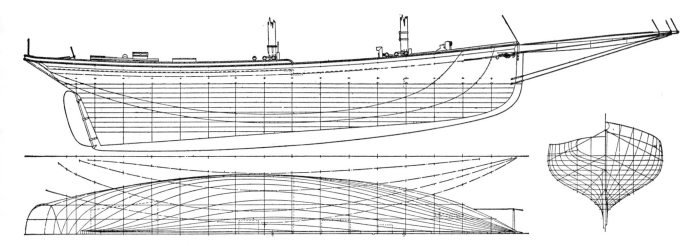

FIGURE 9. *The* Carrie E. Phillips, *1886, which introduced new features of sparring and rigging. Built at Essex, Massachusetts, by Arthur D. Story for Benjamin F. Phillips and Co. of Boston.*

a more rockered keel than had yet been tried in a fisherman; she introduced many new features of masting and rigging, such as the spike bowsprit with a spreader through the stem, a short foremast and improved ironwork. She was one of the first, if not the first, fisherman to have wire standing rigging. There were changes on deck and below as well; the old double hatch forward was dropped, and so were the wooden catheads. Below, the forecastle was lengthened to give greater accommodation. The *Phillips,* in spite of her increased dimensions, was considered a small carrier; she lasted 12 years, "going lost" in August, 1899. This schooner had a big reputation for speed and was noted for her looks.

Among the major changes brought about by the advent of the *Phillips* was the bringing of the headstay to the gammoning iron, resulting in the disappearance of the big jib and the introduction of the modern double-headsail rig. She was, incidentally, one of very few fishing schooners out of New England ports that was painted white, in the yacht fashion, but, naturally, this did not prove very satisfactory.

Though the *Phillips* introduced many of the features seen later in fishermen, it must not be supposed that all schooners built immediately after her were fitted in the same manner. For some years, a number of schooners were built with jib-booms, while those with spike bowsprits often had the forestay a few feet forward of the gammoning iron, and a fairly big jib.

Before going on with the development of the fisherman, it is worth while to describe the painting of these vessels during the early 1880's. The majority of these schooners were painted a bottle or emerald green from water line to waist, the bulwarks above the waist being black and the covebead yellow; the underbody was red copper. On deck, the schooners were usually "dolled up" like the proverbial "little red wagon;" the waterways were blue or chocolate, and large circles were swept in at the foremast bed, at the great beam and at the quarters, the rest of the deck being usually gray, oil or buff. The inboard face of the bulwark stanchions was bright, and the sides were either white or cherry stain; the bottoms were painted with the waterway color. Between the stanchions, the inside of the bulwarks was cherry stained. The tops of hatches and trunk were the same as the waterways. The tops of the main and quarter deck rail caps were often bright, and the sides white. Hatch coamings were either white or gray. Spars were varnished, the masthead was white, as was the bowsprit outside the stem, with the inboard portion black; but if a spike bowsprit was fitted, the whole stick was black. This scheme of painting lasted until about 1894.

The *Phillips* was not followed in hull design by any similar vessel, for in 1889 a new and more taking Burgess design came out. This was the great *Fredonia*, built by Moses Adams, at Essex, for J. Malcolm Forbes of Boston. A sister schooner with slight alterations was also laid down by Adams in a sub-contractor's yard at East Boston for Thomas F. McManus, also of Boston, who was later to become one of the greatest of designers of fishing schooners. This last was the *Nellie Dixon*. Of the two, the *Dixon* was the first to join the fishing fleet, the *Fredonia* being used as a yacht for a year or so. With their graceful clipper stems, rockered keels, easy lines, and speed and handiness, these two schooners were so much admired that the majority of the new vessels following them from the stocks followed them in model. A number of vessels were built from the *Fredonia* molds, and the modelers, such as "Mel" (George M.) McClain, of Rockport, Tom Irving of Gloucester, and Burnham, and Tarr, of Essex, got out designs incorporating many of her features. The *Fredonia* was 109.44 tons net, 99.6 feet long, 23.6 feet beam and 10.3 depth of hold. She foundered on the Banks on December 18, 1896. She introduced no really new features, but represented a refinement of the *Phillips* in a more cutaway forefoot and shorter bowsprit. It is probable that her popularity over the *Phillips* was largely due to her beauty and to the publicity she received on her initial appearance.

One of the points raised against the *Fredonia's* model was the lack of carrying capacity in relation to her length, so the modelers attempted to improve on the model in this feature, at least. Irving and McClain both turned out schooners that acquired great reputations for speed and power. Though they followed the appearance of the *Fredonia* above the water line in a general way, they did not indulge in slavish copying, but departed boldly from the original, working out improvements that seemed desirable. The result was that by 1890 they had developed a type that was popular until well after the turn of the century. The McClain vessels may be taken as illustrations of the new model thus produced. From McClain's models were built such fine schooners as the *Eliza B. Campbell,* in 1890, the *Marguerite Haskins,* in 1893, and *M. Madaleine,* in 1894. McClain had been modeling since 1880, and had acquired a reputation with some of his early bankers, especially with the *Puritan,* in 1887.

The plan of the *Eliza B. Campbell,* Figure 10, shows the features of the class of schooners under discussion. She was built at Essex by Moses Adams for Hodge and Poole, of Gloucester, and measured 95.17 tons net, 88.4 feet long, 23.9 feet beam, and 9.8 feet depth of hold. She was lost in 1901.

The *Campbell* was one of the last vessels built with jibbooms; she had a rather complicated head rigging, using not only whiskers but also the spreader introduced with spike bowsprits. Vessels with this rig were built as late as 1894, but, as a rule, schooners built from 1890 on had the pole bowsprit.

A comparison of the four plans published here, Figures 7, 8, 9, and 10, will show the development that took place during the period we have covered, but the changes that took place in the bows and sterns of fishermen require special mention. In larger vessels the type of stem seen in the *Fears,* with the upper head rail added, gradually went out of use during the early 1880's. The wooden head rails

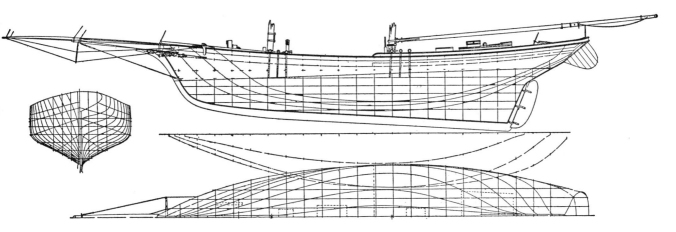

FIGURE 10.  *A representative of the fishing schooners popular until after the turn of the century, the* Eliza B. Campbell, *1890. Built at Essex, Massachusetts, by Moses Adams for Hodge and Poole of Gloucester.*

were replaced by iron rods as braces to the cutwater, and the stem or cutwater knee was greatly shortened.  At the same time, the cheek knees seem to have been omitted, leaving only the "noble wood" (pad at the hawse) and the trail boards. In the late 1880's, the bottom edge of the trail was rounded up at its after end to meet the after edge of the "noble wood."  The result was an effect somewhat like the well-known head of the yacht *America*.  The wooden catheads were retained, their bottoms being rounded off just below the waist line.  It was during the development of this type of cutwater that the plumb or straight stem, such as that of the *Story*, became popular, at first retaining the "noble wood," but dropping it when bowsprit spreaders were introduced through the bows, as in the *Carrie E. Phillips*.  Neither the *America* nor the plumb stems had a long popularity, both giving way to the bald clipper stem of the 1890's.  This stem was merely the old "gammon knee" head, usually having an eagle head or a billet at the fore end, with no trails, the scrolls being cut into the knee and planking.  The bowsprit spreaders went out of use because they were not required with the short bowsprits made possible with the cutaway forefoot that became general in the new schooners of the last of the Nineties.

There was a somewhat similar evolution in the counters of these vessels. The short, wide counter sterns of the 1870's gave way to the longer overhang of the 1880's, which, for a few years, had much competition for popular favor from the deep "V" transom of the pilot boats. Finally, the overhang having retained supremacy, it was gradually lengthened during this period of its development. During the era of the Burgess schooners, the tendency was toward rather short counters with no visible knuckle at the junction of transom and horn timber, but in the 1890's, the transom was set with less rake, in the manner later popular.

Beginning in the last of the Eighties and during the following twenty years, the New England fishing schooner reached its highest development; the fleet was one of which any nation might well be proud.

# 2 / The Mackerel Fishery

## GEORGE BROWN GOODE

THE PURSE-SEINE HAS COME INTO GENERAL USE SINCE 1850, AND WITH its introduction the methods of the mackerel fishery have been totally revolutionized. The most extensive changes, however, have taken place since 1870, for it is only during the last ten years that the use of the purse-seine has been at all universal.

In the spring, from March to the 1st of June, the mackerel seiners cruise between the capes of the Chesapeake and the South Shoal of Nantucket. The mackerel are first encountered off Chesapeake and Delaware Bays, from 20 to 50 miles from the land, and gradually move northward, followed by the fleet. When off the coasts of New Jersey, Long Island, and Block Island, the fish usually draw closer in to land, frequently approaching within 1 or 2 miles of the shore. During the summer and fall months the principal seining ground for mackerel is in the Gulf of Maine, from the Bay of Fundy to Cape Cod; the immediate vicinity of Mount Desert Rock, Matinicus Rock, Monhegan Island, Cape Elizabeth, Boone Island, and Massachusetts Bay being favorite localities. Good catches of mackerel are frequently made in summer on Georges Bank, and, within the past few years, near Block Island.

The mackerel fleet contains a larger percentage of American-born fishermen than any other. The 113 mackerel vessels from Gloucester in 1879 were manned

Excerpted from *The Fisheries and Fishery Industries of the United States*, by George Brown Goode. Taken from Section V, "History and Methods of the Fisheries," Volume I, Part 3, "The Mackerel Fishery of the United States," pages 247-269. This seven-volume work was published by the Government Printing Office in 1887.

131

*The cabin of the mackerel schooner,* John D. Long, *of Gloucester. Drawing by H. W. Elliott.*

by 1,438 men, of whom 821 were Americans; 322 Provincials; 24 British, most of whom were Irish; 39 Scandinavians; 6 French; and 13 Portuguese.

The mackerel fleet in 1880 was made up of four hundred and sixty-eight vessels, which pursued this fishery to a greater or less extent. Of these, two hundred and thirty-five vessels were employed exclusivly in catching mackerel between March and November, though some of the fleet did not start before June or July. A large number of these, the best fishing vessels of New England, in winter are engaged in the haddock fishery, in the Georges fishery, in the herring trade, in the oyster trade, and in the West India fruit trade, as well as in the shore cod fishery.

The mackerel vessels are, as a class, swift sailers; they carry, while engaged in this fishery, all the canvas which their rig will allow. The mackerel schooners,

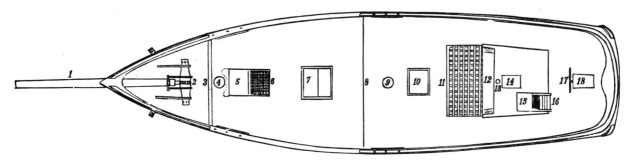

*Deck plan of schooner fitted for mackerel purse-seining: 1, bowsprit; 2, windlass; 3, jib sheet traveller; 4, foremast; 5, fore companion; 6, fore hatch grating; 7, main hatch; 8, break of quarterdeck; 9, mainmast; 10, after hatch; 11, grating for stowing seines; 12, barrel-head box; 13, stove pipe; 14, skylight; 15, cabin companion slide; 16, companion stairs; 17, steering wheel; 18, wheel box. Drawing by Captain J. W. Collins.*

as a rule, spread more sail, in comparison with their size, than any other vessels in the world, except, perhaps, the extreme type of schooner-rigged yacht, which is essentially a development of the fishing schooner.

Vessels designed especially for the work of seining mackerel usually have a wide deck, much deck-room being necessary for the proper handling of the fish. Many of the schooners of 60 to 80 tons have a beam of 21½ feet to 23 feet. But, although plenty of deck-room is considered of great importance to a mackerel vessel, even deck room is held to be less necessary than speed. In consequence, every effort has been made by the builders to construct swift sailing schooners, and the result is that many of the vessels composing the mackerel fleet are able to cope successfully with many yachts of the same size. The mackerel vessel is fitted for seining:

(1)   By placing upon her a summer outfit of repairs and sails.

(2)   By removing the heavy cables used in winter fishing, and substituting chain cables.

(3)   By the removal of gurry-pens, and all other incumbrances from the deck.

(4)   By the rigging of a seine-roller upon the port-quarter rail. This is a

wooden roller almost invariably made of spruce, 6 inches in diameter, and 9 to 10 feet long, which revolves on pivots in its ends, received into iron sockets in cleats, which are fastened to the rail. The forward end of the roller is about 3 feet aft of the main rigging. The use of this roller is to lessen the friction between the rail of the vessel and the seine, as the latter is being hauled on deck or overhauled into the boat.

(5)   By the head-box being fastened to the forward end of the house. The head-box is a bin 10 or 12 feet long, and wide enough to receive the head of a fish barrel. In this box are stowed the heads of the barrels that happen to be on deck.

(6)   By placing the bait-mill on deck, and fastening the bait-box (when one is used) to the main rigging on the starboard side.

(7)   By nailing boards to the top timbers underneath the main rail, between the fore and main rigging; these are about 6 inches in width, and are provided with single ropes, or stoppers, 2 or 3 feet apart; the object of these stoppers is to hold the cork rope of the seine when brought over the rail, preparatory to bailing the fish from the seine upon the deck.

(8)   By taking on board an ice-grinder, these being used only on vessels which carry their fish fresh to market.

(9)   By clearing the hold of all bulkheads, ice-houses, or other appliances, which may have been used in the course of the winter's fishery.

(10)   By properly adjusting the quantity of ballast; if the vessel has been in the haddock or Georges fishery, ballast must be removed; if in the herring trade, ballast must be added; a mackerel schooner of 60 tons will carry from 15 to 20 tons of ballast, and in exceptional cases somewhat more.

(11)   By constructing an ice-house on those vessels which intend to take their fish fresh to market, somewhat similar to that on board the halibut vessels.

(12)   By taking on board the necessary supply of barrels. Vessels which take their fish fresh to market carry from 175 to 250 barrels; those intending to salt their fish carry from 175 to 500 barrels, about one-third of this number being filled with salt, which is used in curing the fish, and serves in the meantime as ballast.

The seine-boat, as now in use, resembles the well-known whale-boat, differing from it, however, in some important particulars. The seine-boat must have three qualities:  (1) It should tow well; consequently it is made sharpest forward.

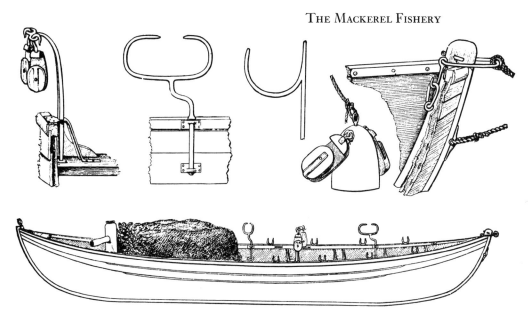

*Seine boat; purse davit and blocks; oar rests; purse weight and purse blocks; and bow fittings.*

A whale-boat, on the other hand, is sharpest aft, to facilitate backing after the whale has been struck. (2) It should row well, and this quality also is obtained by the sharp bow. The whale-boat also should row well, but in this case it has been found desirable to sacrifice speed in part to the additional safety attained by having the stern sharper than the bow. (3) It should be stiff or steady in the water, since the operation of shooting the seine necessitates much moving about in the boat.

The Gloucester seine-boat of the present day is a modification of the old-fashioned whale-boat, combining the qualities mentioned above. The average length of such a boat is about 34 feet, its width 7 feet 5 inches, its depth amidship 33 inches. At the stern is a platform, measuring about 4 feet, fore and aft, on which the captain stands to steer; this is 6 to 8 inches below the gunwale. Another platform extends the whole length of the boat's bottom, from the afterpart of which the seine is set. In the bow is still another platform, on which stands the man who hauls the corkline. There are four thwarts or seats, a large space being left clear behind the middle of the boat for the storage of the seines. Upon the starboard side of the boat, near the middle, is arranged an upright iron support, about 18 inches in height, to which are attached two iron snatch-blocks used in working the purse-ropes. Upon the opposite side of the boat, generally near the bow and stern, but with position varied according to the fancies of the fishermen, are fixed in the gunwale two staples, to which are attached other snatch-blocks used to secure additional purchase upon the purse-ropes. In the center of the platform at the stern of the boat is placed a large wooden pump, used to draw out the water which accumulates in large quantities during the hauling of the seine.

Until 1872 the seine-boats were always built in the lap-streak style; since that time an improved form of smooth-bottomed boats, built with battened seam, set-work, sheathed inside with pine, and with oak frame and pine platform, has been growing in popularity. The advantages claimed for this boat by the builders are: (1) increasing speed; (2) greater durability, on account of the more solid character of the woodwork and tighter seams; and (3) less liability to catch the twine of the nets by reason of the smooth sides. It is not so stiff as a lap-streaked boat of the same width, but in other respects is superior. Seven, eight, or nine oars, usually 13 or 14 feet in length, are used in these boats, besides a steering-oar of 16 or 17.

These boats last, with ordinary usage, six or seven years. At the close of the fishing season they are always taken ashore and laid up for the winter in a shed or under trees, and are completely refitted at the beginning of another season.

The seine-boat is usually towed astern by a warp, a 2½ or 3 inch rope, 20 to 50 fathoms in length. When the vessel is making a long passage the seine-boat is hoisted upon the deck. Most of the larger vessels carry two seine-boats and two seines. On the largest schooners these boats are both of a large size; in other vessels, one of them is usually a small one. In addition to the seine-boats, each vessel carries two dories. One of these is usually towed astern when the vessel is on the fishing grounds; sometimes both. They are taken on deck in rough weather, when making a passage, or when not required for use in fishing. When a large catch is obtained at the last set of a seine for the trip, and more mackerel are secured than the barrels on board will hold, the dories are taken on deck and filled with fish. During the mackerel season it is a common occurrence to see, in any of the large fishing ports, vessels arrive with both dories piled full of mackerel.

Two kinds of seines are used. The large seine, used only in connection with

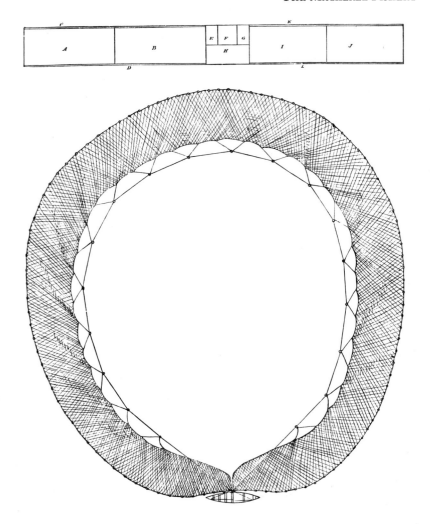

*Top: Diagram showing the different sections of a purse seine: A and J, arms of net; B and I, wings; C, D, K, and L, border of stout twine; F, bailing piece or bunt; E and G, sides; and H, under.*

*Bottom: Diagram showing the form of a purse seine when spread in the water. Drawings by Captain J. W. Collins.*

the largest kind of seine-boat, is 190 to 225 fathoms in length, and 20 to 25 fathoms in depth when it is hung, being deeper in the center of the bunt than at the extreme wings, one of which, the "boat end," is from 1 to 10 fathoms deep, and the other, the "dory end," varies from about 7 to 15 fathoms in depth.

When the vessel is not searching for fish the seine is stowed on a grating forward of the house, between that and the after hatch. When the seine is stowed in the boat or upon the deck, it is always "salted down" to prevent it from rotting or burning. From a bushel to a barrel of salt or more is used, according to the necessity of the case. When the seine is thus stowed, it is often protected by a canvas cover.

When looking out for mackerel the seines are generally stowed in the seine boats upon the platform arranged for that purpose between the two after thwarts. The cork-lines are stowed aft and the lead-lines forward, the seine always being set from the starboard side of the boat.

The seine is always passed from the boat to the vessel, and vice versa, over the roller upon the port side, which has already been described. To transfer the seine from the vessel to the boat requires five or more men. The operation can be performed in from 15 to 30 minutes. To haul the wet seine from the boat to the vessel is a somewhat laborious task, but as less care is required than in stowing it in the boat, less time is usually needed to perform this operation.

Mackerel seiners usually carry a small supply of bait for the purpose of tolling the fish to the surface and, incidentally, of catching fish with the jigs when they are not schooling. Sometimes they toll the school alongside and spread the seine around the vessel, and after she sails over the cork-rope and away to leeward, the net is pursed up and the fish captured. It is often the case, too, when mackerel are moving rapidly, for the men in the dory to throw bait ahead of the school, and while the fish are thus induced to stop, the seine-boat circles around them, the net is thrown out and while yet engaged in feeding, the fish are enclosed in the big purse. Many good catches are obtained in this way. The favorite bait is slivered and salted menhaden, of which each vessel carries 5 to 10 barrels when they can be procured. Most of the vessels, however, at the present time, depend entirely upon small mackerel, which they catch and salt.

The following description of the method of seining mackerel is mainly from the pen of Mr. J. P. Gordy: When a vessel is on the fishing grounds and there are no signs of fish, if the weather is favorable, a man is stationed at the mast-head on the lookout, while the rest of the crew, excepting, of course, the man at the wheel, lounge lazily around, amusing themselves as they feel inclined. If a whale is seen blowing or a vessel is "putting out her boat," the man at the wheel steers toward them. The skipper is usually on deck directing the evolutions of the vessel, and is consulted before any change is made in the course of the vessel. When signs of fish begin to be numerous, and sea geese and gannets are plenty, and whales and porpoises show themselves frequently, the "fishy men" of the crew stop lounging and begin to survey the surface of the water intently. At such times one can count half a dozen here and there in the rigging, carefully observing the movements of other vessels, if any of the fleet are in sight. "There's crooked actions, men," the skipper exclaims, meaning that some vessel in sight suddenly alters her course, and that she is either on fish herself or sees another vessel that is. When one school appears, another is likely to be seen, and when a vessel has "crooked actions," those who observe them bend their course in the direction in which she is sailing. When a man sees fish, he shouts, "I see a school." "Where?" asks the captain. The direction is indicated. "How does it look; is it a good one?" He wants to know whether they are tinkers or whether the fish seem large. If they are abundant he will wait until he gets a "sight" at a good school. Much attention is paid by the lookouts to the manner in which the school of fish is moving. The seiners prefer those schools which are "cart wheeling," or going round and round in circles in a compact body, in the act of feeding. Fish which are "cart wheeling" can be surrounded with a seine much more readily than those going straight ahead in one direction.

If the man who has found the school is not experienced, the captain examines it for himself, and if satisfied that it is a good one he shouts, "Get in the seine-boat; look alive, boys." As a pack of school-boys jump from an apple tree when the indignant owner appears, so eleven men leap into the seine-boat one over another, as if they had meant to jump overboard but by accident had reached the seine-boat instead. The captain takes his place at the steering-oar. Two men sit on the forward part of the seine and one at the cork-line, ready to "throw out the twine" when the captain gives the word of command. The remaining seven row swiftly and silently until the fish disappear or the captain orders them to "stop

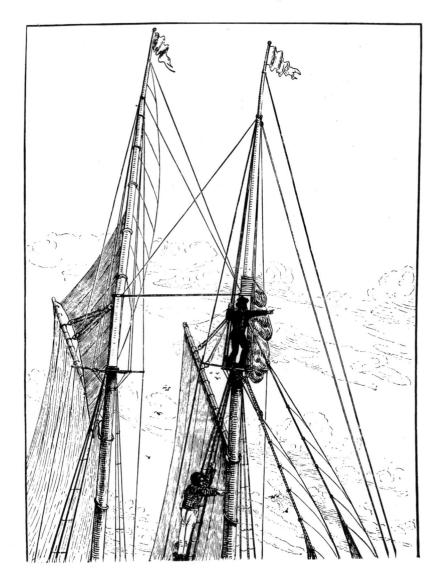

*Lookouts aloft in a schooner on the watch for mackerel. Drawing by H. W. Elliott and Captain J. W. Collins.*

rowing." All the while the captain is eagerly watching the fish, noticing which way they move and how fast. Before beginning to put out his twine, he wants to get near enough to enable him to make the wings of the seine meet around the school. He must, therefore, keep far enough away to prevent the head of the school from striking the seine until it is nearly pursed up. He calculates the speed of the fish, and sets the seine in such a manner that by the time the school gets thoroughly within the circle of the net he will be able to come around to the starting point and completely encircle them. If he fails in this, the wings of the seine must be towed together before it can be pursed up, and in the time thus occupied there is a chance of losing the fish. A skillful skipper rarely fails in making the ends of the seine meet. In seining on Georges, or any other place where there is a strong tide, it requires much skill and judgment to set the seine in such a manner that it shall not be tripped and thrown out upon the surface of the water. Under these circumstances, to prevent "tripping," the seine should be so set that the bunt of it will be in the direction from which the tide runs; the force of the tide then aiding the act of pursing the net.

When the skipper is near enough to satisfy the conditions of the above problems he orders the men at the seine to "put out the twine." They begin their work, the oarsmen in the meantime rowing as fast as possible. The skipper steers the boat around the school in such a manner that when the seine is fully out the cork-line approximates more or less closely to the form of a circle. Two of the men who did not get in the seine-boat now appear on the scene of action in the dory in which they have closely followed in the wake of the seine-boat until the act of setting begins. As soon as the first end of the seine has been thrown overboard they row up to it and seize the buoy at the end of the cork-line, which they hold until the seine-boat has made a circle, merely rowing fast enough to keep the end of the seine in its place and to prevent it from swagging. When the seine-boat has completed its circle, it approaches the dory, which is holding fast to the buoy. When the two ends of the seine meet, the men in the dory get into the seine-boat to assist in pursing; sometimes, however, the ends do not meet, and in this case they are brought together by means of a line, about 20 fathoms in length, which is always taken in the dory and is fastened by the men in the dory to the buoy and carried to the seine-boat.

*"Paying out" the seine. Drawing by H. W. Elliott and Captain J. W. Collins.*

The work of "pursing up" is now to be performed with all possible speed. Until this is begun the seine is in the form of a hollow cylinder, and the fish, in order to escape, have only to dive down and swim away under the lead-line. In pursing, the bottom of the seine is to be closed up, and in this operation the saying of the men, "A man who won't pull every pound he can and an ounce more is not fit to be a fisherman," is fully exemplified.

The men stand six in one end of the seine-boat and seven in the other end, holding the two ends of the purse-line, which, having passed through the rings in the bridles on the lead-line of the seine, pass round the two blocks of the purse-davit and through the snatch-blocks on the opposite side of the seine-boat, one of which is forward and the other aft. One of the uses of the bridles now appears. As soon as the men in the seine-boat commence pursing up the seine, the rings, which before this have been hanging downward below the lead-line, now extend the same distance laterally from this line. We have only to remember that they all extend toward each other to see that they considerably diminish the open area at the bottom of the seine. To be sure, the spaces between the bridles are open, but the fish are not likely to escape through these, for in such an attempt many of them would strike the bridles and finding such obstacles would turn, hoping to find an outlet in some other direction.

As previously remarked, the seine before being pursed up is in the shape of a hollow cylinder. A strong tide may make it take the form of a hollow frustum with a slit in its side. Its longer area is at the bottom. In such a case the slit is wider at the bottom and grows narrower toward the top, until it vanishes at a point where the two ends of the purse-line bring the seine together at the purse-davit. Then the purse weight comes into play. This is "reeved out" to the two end lines, and its weight brings the two ends of the seine together, closing up the

*"Pursing the seine." Drawing by H. W. Elliott and Captain J. W. Collins.*

slit and destroying the frustum shape of the seine. If this were not done the fish might escape at the side as well as at the bottom.

When the seine is pursed up it is in the form of a bag, the bottom of which does not hang freely, for it is bent upward, having been drawn up by the purse-line near the side of the boat, and during the operation of pursing up the boat is pulled nearly into the center of the circle made by the corks on the upper edge of the seine. Occasionally, when there is a current, the boat is brought up against the corks in the bunt of the seine. The object is now to get the fish, if they have any, into such close quarters that they may be taken on deck. To do this the larger part of the seine must be pulled into the seine-boat and this operation, called "drying up," now begins. The seine is taken up entirely if there be no fish, partly if the school has not escaped, and the net is so drawn up that the "bailing-piece" will in-close the fish at last. The position of this part of the seine being marked by the central cork it is of course not difficult to bring it around the fish. The experienced fishermen can also quickly tell, either night or day, when the bunt of the seine is reached in the process of drying up, since the difference in the size of the twine of which the bailing-piece is made and that of the other parts of the net is readily detected.

If any fish have been caught, especially if the school is large, the skipper and three or four men go in the dory to the vessel to help the cook, who is the only man on board, to bring her alongside of the seine-boat. If the school is very large the dory is rowed to the vessel as rapidly as possible, and the second dory is rowed back to the seine for the purpose of holding up the bunt, since a school of 500 barrels may sink both seine and seine-boat if left without assistance. This, how-ever, rarely occurs, and it generally happens that the school either is small enough to be dipped into the dory and to be taken to the vessel, or that the seine boat without any assistance is capable of managing them until the vessel is brought alongside.

While the fish are being caught the cook has charge of the vessel; if it hap-pens to be about meal time he attends to the cooking as best he can, but whether the cakes burn or not the vessel must be cared for, and he generally divides his time between the forecastle and the wheel. If he is preparing dinner and is able to, he continues his cooking, taking charge of the vessel at the same time.

*Bailing mackerel from the purse seine. Drawing by H. W. Elliott and Captain J. W. Collins.*

The vessel usually "lays to," with the jib to windward, not far from the seine-boat; and perhaps, as the cook sits at the wheel, he has a basin of potatoes before him, which he peels while he is eagerly watching every movement of the seine-boat, trying to ascertain whether his mates are successful, and, if so, to what degree.

When the dory has been rowed aboard, the men at once take measures to bring the vessel alongside of the seine-boat. The evolution of shooting alongside of a seine-boat calls into play all the skill of the steersman. The vessel must approach so near that a rope may be thrown to the men in the seine-boat, and in such a manner that she will move slowly enough not to tear the seine as it is pulled along, before the schooner is "bowsed to the windward" and her motion ceases.

The cork-line is then taken over the side of the vessel and made fast by "stoppers" along the rail. This having been done the process of drying up is resumed, and the fish are gathered together in a compact body so that they can be dipped out upon the deck. When the fish are to be taken on deck the men are

145

distributed as follows: Three or four are employed in hoisting the fish by means of a large dip-net attached to the main and forestaysail halyards; the captain directs the movements of the net, holding its long handle, and shouting "Hoist!" when it is about half full of fish. Two men standing by the rail empty the dip-net on the deck.

When all the fish have been bailed out the seine is overhauled and salted. In the mean time most of the crew are making preparations to dress the fish. If the school is large, the crew, cook and all, unless it is just at meal time, begin the work as soon as the fish are ready; if the catch of fish is small, and there is a prospect of getting another set that day, a part of the crew take the seine out of the seine-boat to mend it, if necessary, and lay it back in an orderly form so that it may be thrown out without difficulty.

The operation of setting a seine around the school and pursing it up usually occupies from ten to twelve minutes, though it is claimed by some expert fishermen that they have done it in seven minutes. Under unfavorable circumstances it may be nearly an hour from the time the first end is thrown out until the "pursings" are on the boat. This delay is usually caused by a strong tide, such as is generally found on Georges. The catch of a purse-seine may vary from one barrel to five or six hundred barrels. The seine may be set eight or ten times in the course of a day without getting any considerable quantity, or perhaps no fish, the mackerel escaping by diving under the "lead-line"; and then a more fortunate set will secure more fish than can by any possibility be taken care of by the crew of the vessel. Under such circumstances it is customary to set a flag from the main-topmast head or main peak. This is to indicate to vessels which may be in sight that more fish have been caught than can be taken care of, and that the skipper is willing to dispose of some of them. This is called "giving the seine away." Sometimes the fish are given away to be dressed on shares, and at other times they are given away without expectation of return. An ordinary crew can dress and salt at one time about 100 barrels of small mackerel or 200 barrels of large ones.

Very large quantities of fish can be taken care of in a short time. Vessels have been known to leave New York on one day and return the next day with 200 to 300 barrels of fresh mackerel, while some Gloucester vessels in the course of a week have caught and salted 500 to 600 barrels, landing two or three cargoes during that time.

It sometimes happens that, when a large school of mackerel has been taken in a seine, the fish press down so hard on the bottom of the net that the fishermen find it difficult, if not impossible, to gather in on the twine sufficiently to "dry the fish up" enough to bring them to the surface. It has been found, however, that by throwing coal ashes into the water alongside of the seine the fish are caused to rise to the surface, being frightened by the whitish appearance which the ashes give to the sea. When the mackerel rise the twine can be readily drawn in.

As is well known to all who are familiar with the sea, the water, on dark nights, frequently exhibits a remarkably brilliant phosphorescent display. At such times objects moving in the sea can be distinctly traced by the illumination which they leave behind, and schools of fish rising near the surface can be readily seen. Indeed, on some occasions so remarkable is the phosphorescence thrown out from a large school of fish that it frequently seems to light up the surrounding darkness. From this reason, and the fact that the fishermen, by long experience and close observation, can accurately determine the kind of fish which he may see sporting at night, he is thus often enabled to learn the whereabouts of certain species, such, for instance, as the mackerel and their abundance, even when they do not come to the surface during the day. The mackerel is a remarkably capricious fish, and perhaps for many days in succession its presence cannot be detected in its favorite haunts while daylight lasts, and the fisherman therefore seeks for it in vain, but as soon as the sun sets and darkness appears over the sea the schools rise to the surface and the fish continue to disport themselves in this manner until near daylight, when they again sink out of sight.

For many years after the introduction of purse-seines it was considered impracticable by the fishermen to catch mackerel in the night, but at last some of the more adventurous skippers, having a favorable opportunity for night fishing, and deeming it possible to catch the mackerel, made an attempt and met with even better success than they dared to anticipate. Thereafter they followed up this method of fishing whenever a good chance occurred, but as it usually resulted greatly to their personal success, as well as increased their reputation among their fellow fishermen, on account of the additional amount of fish caught, they were by no means anxious to tell that part of their catch was made in the night, since, if they did so, all the other mackerel fishermen would at once come directly into competition with them. As a matter of course, however, the fact of mackerel being seined at night could not long be kept a secret, and the result was that one after another began to adopt this practice until in the fall of 1881 it reached its climax, nearly every vessel in the fleet engaging to a greater or less extent in night fishing.

The method of seining mackerel in the night is as follows: The vessel being on the fishing-ground, if the night is favorable, she is allowed to sail slowly ahead while a man goes aloft to the foremast-head and keeps a lookout for the fish. If the signs are peculiarly favorable, perhaps two or more men may be aloft for this purpose. These lookouts are the men who have the watch on deck, and, not infrequently, the skipper may be one of them, his ambition to succeed often impelling him to remain up during the entire night, constantly keeping on the alert for fish and watching the movements of surrounding vessels. The remainder of the crew—those having a watch below—are thoroughly prepared and dressed in their oil-clothes ready to jump into the seine-boat at a moment's warning. If the fish are not seen in the first of the night, the men off duty lie down on the cabin forecastle floors or stretch themselves on the lockers, and endeavor in this way to get what sleep they can, unless, indeed, they may be busy on deck in caring for the fish taken the night or day previous. When a school of fish is seen by the lookout, he at once shouts "I see a school!" If it is the skipper who first descries them, he gives directions to the man at the wheel how to steer in order to approach them. If not, the man who first reports the school is asked in which direction it bears from the vessel. He also directs how the course shall be laid in order to approach close to the body of fish. In the meantime the men below, having been hurriedly awakened, rush on deck and quickly take their places in the seine-boat and dory which are towed alongside or astern. If the mackerel "show up" well and can be plainly seen by the men in the boat, the latter is cast off as soon as the vessel approaches close to the school, and the seine is set and pursed up in the same manner as has before been described; though it frequently happens that, owing to the darkness of the night, it is quite difficult to bring the ends of the net together with such a degree of certainty and success as it is generally done in the daytime. Of late, however, the custom of carrying a light in the dory has been adopted in order that the skipper, who steers the boat, may determine the position of the end of the seine first put out and therefore be enabled to make a circle with a great deal more accuracy than he otherwise could. It often happens that fish can only be seen by the man at the mast-head, and in such cases the vessel is usually hove to near the mackerel, and the lookout directs the men in the boat how to row in order to surround the school. Another method, we are told, has been occasionally adopted when the chance for its success is promising. If the wind is sufficiently moderate the lookout at the foremast-head may direct the course of the vessel in such a manner that nearly a complete circle may be made round the school of fish. In this case the seine-boat remains fastened to the stern and is towed along by the vessel while the men in her throw out the seine in obedience to the order given by the man at the mast-head. At the proper time she is cast off and proceeds to close up the circle by bringing together the ends of the seine. The dory is cast off and allowed to remain at the end of the seine as usual until the other end is brought around her. An evolution of this kind, of course, requires the most skillful seaman-ship for its success, and also remarkable qualities of adaptability in the vessel.

A lantern is carried both in the seine-boat and dory, the one in the former always being kept darkened or out of sight until the seine is set, since a light would so blind the men in the boat that it would be difficult for them to perform success-fully the work of setting the net.

When a school of mackerel has been taken in the seine and the net is pursed up, a signal is made by the crew of the seine-boat, who have a lantern, so as to attract the attention of the men on board of the vessel, who immediately bring the latter near the seine-boat. The skipper and three or four of the crew then go on board the vessel in the dory and bring the schooner alongside the seine-boat, per-forming this evolution in the same manner as it is done in the daytime. The lantern, which is always carried in the seine-boat, enables the skipper to find her without any trouble. Much vexatious delay and difficulty, however, sometimes occurs in consequence of the light carried by the seine-boat's crew being extin-guished. In such case it is not only hard, but sometimes impossible for the men on the vessel to find the seine-boat, since on a dark, windy night she cannot be seen more than a few rods distant.

It is claimed that the practice of using a large lantern to attract the fish nearer to the surface of the water than they usually come, so that they can be more plainly seen, has met with decided success, and it is believed that there is reason for anticipating considerable improvements in this respect hereafter. In alluding to this matter a writer in the *Cape Ann Advertiser*, November 4, 1881, says:

"It would not greatly surprise us if the mackerel fleet, next year, were supplied with powerful calcium lights, to be carried at the masthead, and that the fishery will be extensively prosecuted in the nighttime. Surely the signs of progression are manifest in almost every branch of the fisheries, and brains are rapidly coming to the front and making themselves manifest. A year ago who would have dreamed of catching mackerel in the nighttime? Now it is fast becoming a reality."

As may be readily inferred, this practice of night fishing is one which calls for great endurance and hardihood on the part of the fishermen who engage in it. It frequently happens, when good catches are made for days and nights in succession, that the men get no rest whatever until they are thoroughly worn out by their constant labors and vigils and are scarcely able to refrain from falling asleep even when engaged at their work. Nor is the work on the fishing ground all they have to do. When a fare is obtained, all sail is made upon the vessel and she is driven as swiftly as possible for the home port, where the fish are landed, new supplies taken on board, and again the men go to sea without, in the meantime, having an opportunity of visiting their homes or of securing the rest they so much stand in need of. So sharp is the competition in this fishery, and so eager are the fishermen to "make hay while the sun shines," that is, to improve every opportunity during the short season while the mackerel can be taken, that the only limit to their labors is when nature is no longer able to sustain the extraordinary drafts that are made upon it. The following notes written by Capt. S. J. Martin will serve to give an idea of the continued labor and consequent fatigue which the fishermen endure:

"Our mackerel fishermen have 'drove business' this season. I know a number of cases where vessels have arrived in the morning with 300 barrels of mackerel, have landed the fish and gone out again the same night. The schooner *Fleetwing* caught 210 barrels of mackerel; came into Gloucester with them all on deck; hired twenty men who had the fish all dressed and salted at two o'clock the following morning. The vessel's crew went home to sleep; went out again the same morning at eight o'clock.

"Schooner *William M. Gaffney* came in here with 450 barrels of mackerel,

*Mackerel pocket, or spiller, shipped at sea. Drawing by H. W. Elliott and Captain J. W. Collins.*

of which 150 barrels were fresh on deck. The men had not been to sleep for two days and nights, and were nodding while putting the mackerel in the barrels. They got the mackerel all salted at four o'clock in the afternoon. Captain Smith then told the men to go home and rest till morning, but to be down the first thing after breakfast, as he wanted to get the mackerel out and go to sea in the evening. This they did."

In 1877 the schooner *Alice*, of Swan's Island, had a bag-net made of haddock ganging-line, into which the fish were transferred when there were too many to be cared for at once.

A development of this idea is the mackerel pocket or spiller, patented in April, 1880, by H. E. Willard, of Portland, Me., an article long needed in the mackerel seine-fishery, and which has received from the fishermen the name of "mackerel pocket" or "spiller." It was first used by the patentee in 1878; and Capt. George Merchant, Jr., of Gloucester, Mass., invented and put into practical operation an improved spiller in 1880, though it was not until the succeeding summer that the advantage of its use was known to the majority of the mackerel fishermen, who have hastened to adopt it, and now all of the mackerel vessels sailing from this port are provided with one of the pockets.

The apparatus is a large net-bag, 36 feet long, 15 feet wide, and 30 feet deep. It is made of stout, coarse twine, and is attached to the side of the vessel, where it is kept in position, when in use, by wooden poles or "outriggers," which extend out a distance of 15 feet from the schooner's rail.

When distended in this manner, a spiller will hold over 200 barrels of mackerel, which can thus be kept alive, as in the well of a smack, until the crew, who have captured them in the great purse-seines, have time to cure their catch. As is well known, it frequently happens that several hundred barrels of mackerel are taken at a single haul. Heretofore, when such a large quantity of fish were caught, but a comparatively small portion of them could be cured by the crew of the vessel to which the seine belonged. Now when a large school of mackerel are caught in a seine the fish are turned into the bag, from which they are "bailed out" on to the schooner's deck only as fast as they can be dressed, and in this way it frequently happens that a full fare may be secured in a single set of the net. The introduction of this simple net-bag undoubtedly saves to our fishing fleet many thousands of barrels of mackerel each season.

The common method of dressing on a seining schooner is as follows: The men engaged in dressing are divided into gangs generally of three men each. Each gang has two wooden trays about 3 feet square and 6 or 8 inches deep; these are placed on the tops of barrels; one is called a 'gib-tub,' the other a 'splitting-tub.'

One man of each gang splits, the other two gib, or eviscerate, the fish. The tub of the man who splits, of course, contains the fish to be split. With a scoop-net the splitter, or one of the "gibbers," from time to time, fills the splitting-tub from the pile of mackerel lying upon the deck. On the side of the splitting-tray next to the "gibbers" is a board about 6 to 10 inches wide, called a "splitting-board," on which the splitter places the fish as he cuts them open. He takes them in his left hand (on which he has a mitten) round the center of the body, head from him, and with the splitting-knife splits them down the center of the back. As fast as he splits the fish he tosses them into the tray of the "gibbers." The "gibbers" protect their hands with gloves or mittens. As fast as the "gibbers" remove the viscera, with a peculiar double motion of the thumb and fingers of the right hand, they throw the fish into barrels, which are partially filled with water; these are called "wash-barrels." If the men have time they "plow" the fish before salting them, making a gash in the sides of the fish nearly to the skin with the peculiar knife, "the plow," provided for the purpose.

Before the fish are salted the dirty water is poured out and clean water is added. About one barrel of salt is used for every four barrels of mackerel. This is the first salting. When the fish have been salted they are placed in unheaded barrels until the weather is unfit for fishing, or the deck is filled with them, when they are carefully headed up and stowed away below.

The speed with which a large deck-load of mackerel can be disposed of by the crew is something marvelous. A good splitter will handle from forty-five to sixty mackerel a minute. In one well-authenticated case a man split sixty-seven mackerel a minute for three consecutive minutes. A good "gibber" can handle a barrel of large mackerel in from five to seven minutes. A smart crew of fourteen men can dispose of a deck-load of large mackerel in from fifteen to eighteen hours, salting them away properly in the barrels. The smaller the mackerel the longer it takes to dress a barrel of them, the time required to handle a small or a large mackerel being precisely the same.

When the fish are to be iced and carried fresh to market they can be disposed of much more rapidly, it being simply necessary to stow them away in the hold without splitting. They are usually washed before being placed in ice, and occasionally gibbed without splitting, the viscera being drawn through the gill openings. The most rapid way of caring for the fish is to place them in barrels of ice-water. This is done for the most part in the spring or fall.

Those mackerel schooners engaged in market fishing find it desirable to make their passages with the utmost speed, but rapid passages in summer are, of course, much less dangerous than those made in winter by the haddock and halibut vessels. Great expedition is used by all mackerel vessels, since the season is short, and they feel obliged to take advantage of every opportunity. In the case of salted fish, however, there is no such anxiety to sell, and the chief desire of the skipper is to land his fish and to return to the fishing ground with no unnecessary loss of time.

It often happens that mackerel catchers who are not engaged in the fresh-fish trade take a big haul, 200 barrels or so, when they have but few barrels to put them in and scarcely any salt. In such cases it is of the highest importance to reach home if possible, or at least some large fishing port where barrels and salt can be obtained, and all the sail that can be spread or that the vessel will carry is set.

The mackerel are hoisted out on the wharf by a horse, the duty of the crew being to hook on the barrels and to roll them to the proper places on the wharf, after they are landed, where the barrels are generally stowed on their heads, ready to be opened. In seasons of abundance, and when the men have become exceedingly fatigued from their labors in catching and dressing a fare of mackerel, it is often the case that the skipper will hire a number of longshoremen to take the fish out of the vessel. At such times, too, the shoresmen are employed to plow the fish, and also to assist in packing them, since the fishermen find it more profitable to hire men to do this than to remain ashore and do it themselves. For in the meantime they may be fortunate enough to catch a fare of two or three hundred barrels of mackerel.

The following tables, copied from the annual reports of the Boston Fish Bureau, show the large catches and "stocks" by the mackerel fleet in New England waters for the seasons of 1880 and 1881:

| Vessels | Barrels Cured | Amount of stock |
|---|---|---|
| 1880 | | |
| Schooner Alice, Capt. H. B. Joyce, Swan's Island, Me. ........................ | 3,700 | $19,548 75 |
| Schooner Edward E. Webster, Capt. S. Jacobs, Gloucester, Mass. ................. | 3,969 | 19,465 00 |
| Schooner Alice C. Fox, Captain Rowe, Portland, Me. ........... | | 13,432 00 |
| Schooner Louis and Rosa ................................ | 2,769 | 12,492 00 |
| Schooner Frank Butler ................................ | 2,036 | 11,600 00 |

|  | Barrels Cured | Amount of stock |
|---|---|---|
| Schooner Mary Greenwood | 1,700 | $11,035 00 |
| Schooner Kate Florence | 2,500 | 11,000 00 |
| Schooner Addie F. Cole | 1,900 | 10,500 00 |
| Schooner Cora Lee | 1,875 | 10,250 00 |
| Schooner Cora Smith | 2,150 | 10,000 00 |
| Schooner M. O. Curtis | 2,000 | 10,000 00 |
| Schooner Mary Snow | 1,352 | 9,281 00 |
| Schooner F. F. Nickerson | 2,350 | 9,730 00 |
| Schooner Dictator | 1,652 | 9,213 00 |
| Schooner Morning Star | 1,527 | 9,087 00 |

## Vessels
### 1881

|  | Barrels Cured | Amount of stock |
|---|---|---|
| Schooner Alice, Swan's Island, Me. | 4,905 | $28,055 23 |
| Schooner Edward E. Webster, Gloucester, Mass. | 4,500 | 26,570 00 |
| Schooner Isaac Rich, Swan's Island, Me. | 3,276 | 15,500 00 |
| Schooner Frank Butler, Boston, Mass. | 2,600 | 15,000 00 |
| Schooner Mertie and Delmar, South Chatham, Mass. | 3,005 | 14,138 00 |
| Schooner A. E. Herrick, Swan's Island, Me. | 2,280 | 13,674 00 |
| Schooner Robert Pettis, Wellfleet, Mass. | 2,580 | 12,419 18 |
| Schooner Roger Williams, North Haven, Me. | 2,450 | 12,000 00 |
| Schooner R. J. Evans, Harwichport, Mass. | 3,000 | 12,000 00 |
| Schooner Louis and Rosa, Boothbay, Me. | 3,028 | 11,557 46 |

When it is taken into consideration that these vessels are employed in fishing barely eight months at the longest, and some of them only four to six months, it will be seen that the business is an exceedingly profitable one for many of the fleet, while the greater portion make fair returns.

# 3 / *New England Coasting Schooners*

## CHARLES S. MORGAN

The employment of small fore-and-aft-rigged sailing vessels for Atlantic coastwise transportation dates back to the earliest years of our country. Such vessels were handy, economical, easily built of readily accessible materials, perfectly suited to their task, and their number was legion. They were the errand boys, the short-haul freight droghers, and the passenger buses for many a year, and their contribution to coastal community life, especially in New England, was substantial.

Prior to the Civil War our shipbuilding industry and foreign commerce flourished as Yankee clippers were to be seen in every port around the globe. But this happy situation came to an end as the result of the destructive effects of the War and the diversion of popular attention as well as financial capital from maritime affairs to industrial development, westward expansion, and railroad building. Paradoxically, the same forces that virtually ruined our deepwater fleet created demands for bulk cargo transportation, leading to a tremendous expansion of our coastwise fleet and a new lease on life for the wooden shipbuilding industry.

Coastal shipping had always occupied a special, favored position. One of the first acts of Congress in 1789 was the exclusion of foreign vessels from our coastwise transportation. This was perhaps not the result of purely protectionist philosophy towards shipping itself, so much as recognition of the vital cohesive

Reprinted from *The American Neptune* for January 1963 by permission of the author and the Peabody Museum of Salem.

force represented by water-borne interstate commerce in our young nation.

Sailing vessels in the coastwise trades were not subject to the same early competitive pressure of steamers. Not until 1894 did steam tonnage exceed sail tonnage in our coastal shipping. By 1900 our coastwise fleet represented five times our deepwater tonnage, and what is more, forty-six percent of it was in sailing vessels.[1]

It was the vastly expanding demand for lumber, for coal, and for ice, all resulting from urban and suburban development, that called for more and larger coasting schooners. One has only to look at the dwellings and tenements built during the last quarter of the nineteenth century and still to be seen in some of our cities to realize that in late Victorian gingerbread and gimcrack architecture nobody used one piece of lumber where three or four could be made to do. And as people flocked to our cities in the Seventies and Eighties, the building of homes, tenements, shops, and factories consumed vast quantities of lumber. This was brought in schooners from the South and from Maine to every seaport city. This demand for lumber created in turn a new demand for schooners, and this produced logically an increasing demand for southern ship timber. So it went round and round.

The discovery that ice could be shipped great distances and with great profit led to a thriving and highly lucrative trade between Penobscot and Kennebec ports and the urban centers to the South. Scores, probably hundreds of schooners loaded cargoes at icehouses that eventually lined both sides of the Kennebec above Richmond and carried them to the West Indies and every southern port. This shipment of ice, soon almost entirely in schooners, grew from some 30,000 tons in 1860 to 3,000,000 tons in 1890. Twenty years later the export ice trade had all but vanished from Maine. It has been said that in Maine as they made hay in the summer, so they made ice in the winter. It was both a crop and an industry and it kept a large fleet of vessels busy.[2] When it is realized that the average ice cargo may have been about 350 tons, it will be appreciated that a very considerable fleet indeed must have been employed.

A growing demand for lime and building stone was another factor in the postwar growth of coastal shipping. A specialized fleet of tight little two-masted schooners came into being to haul lime from such places as Rockland and Thomaston to Boston, New York, and other coastal cities, where it was used in building mortar. In that day Portland cement was unknown, and the demand for lime consequently enormous. Similarly there was in our expanding society an increased need for stone for public buildings, monuments, breakwaters, roads and curbings. The production of granite was a leading Maine industry for years. Many schooners were kept busy in this rough and heavy work, including a lot of old vessels too decrepit to be acceptable for more attractive cargoes. "It was a common remark that when a vessel got too old for even lumber coasting out of Bangor or carrying wood for the Rockland lime kilns, she was considered none too ripe for the stone business and was often loaded to the scuppers with paving or huge blocks of granite."[3]

The economic force which exercised the most profound influence on schooners was the ever-increasing demand throughout New England for coal. This swelling of coal consumption came about as a result of the expansion of New England railroads, which required larger and larger quantities of fuel, and the enormous increase in the use of electricity, with consequent requirement of coal for steam-driven electrical generators. New England mills, no longer able to operate efficiently on water power, turned to electricity. Street railways gave up the horsecars and went to electric-driven trolley cars. Homes and public buildings and even public streets went from gas illumination to the incandescent lamp. All this required more and more coal, and schooners were the economical means of transportation from the coal ports of Hampton Roads, the Chesapeake, and the Delaware.[4]

Prior to 1850 most schooners registered less than 100 tons and only a relatively small number registered as much as 150 tons. As the demand grew for larger vessels, calling for larger spars, larger sails, and heavier gear, it is not surprising that some enterprising builder of schooners determined to add a third mast. The identity of the first three-masted or tern schooner is uncertain. The rig was known as early as 1801, if not earlier, for on the third of March that year "the American three-masted schooner *Success*" was reported at Kingston, Jamaica, bound to San Domingo. Several other three-masters are known to have existed during the beginning years of the nineteenth century. They came into being in a search for greater speed during a period of war, and size or carrying capacity were no factors in their design. It is apparent that they were not widely known, and after the Treaty of Ghent brought peace in 1815, they were forgotten.

We know that in 1827 the three-masted schooner *Pocahontas* was built in Matthews County, Virginia. She was a double-decked vessel of 380 tons. Her iron bar shrouds and link stays excited much comment wherever she went.[5] Maine shipbuilders rediscovered the rig in the 1830's, and, as Maine came to be the principal schooner-building state, it is not surprising that claims of originality were made by certain Maine towns. Among the early three-masters were *Aurora*, 147 tons, built at Ellsworth, Maine (1831); *Savage*, 173 tons, built at Eden, Maine (1833); *Horse*, 140 tons, built at Bristol, Maine (1833); and *Magnolia*, 83 tons, built at Blue Hill, Maine (1833). These vessels, unlike later examples of the rig, probably carried a square foretopsail and had masts of unequal length. It was during the 1850's that the rig became more or less standardized along lines best remembered today with no square sails and masts of equal length.

In his *Queens of the Western Ocean*, Carl Cutler provides a list of some 127 schooners of 300 tons and upwards built in the United States between 1850 and 1860. No less than forty-four three-masters are included.

During the early years, two different hull forms came into being; a deep-keel model and a shoal model equipped with a centerboard. It was during the 1870's that a compromise hull form became popular; a deep centerboard model which combined many of the sailing advantages of its predecessors.[6]

Anyone who has sailed small boats thinks of a centerboard as a device of small proportions which is lowered beneath the keel of the craft to help her sailing qualities and minimize the leeway she makes. Few realize that centerboards were employed in the majority of three-masters built before 1895, in a great many four-masters, and even in the first five-master. The dimensions of these centerboards became quite formidable. Thirty feet wide and eight inches in thickness was common in the larger schooners; twenty-six feet wide and five or six inches thick in the smaller three-masters. Much as they improved sailing qualities, they were not an unalloyed blessing, because the centerboard well or box occupied valuable cargo space and eventually became a source of leaks, since it was impossible to paint its interior surfaces. In many schooners the centerboards were eventually removed to the detriment of their sailing qualities. Before the turn of the century, large schooner hulls were of a form and draft to make the centerboard unnecessary and their installation was abandoned.

As schooners grew in size and response to utilitarian demands, some coarsening of the lines inevitably followed. The vessels were built full and flat through the mid-section and the ends were shortened. The cargo capacity was thereby increased at the expense of speed and maneuverability. But the fastest vessels were not necessarily the most profitable, and the additional freight money on a few extra tons of capacity could be important.

While it is quite true that schooners by the nature of their rig and the prevailing winds along our shores were best suited to coastwise voyages, let nobody imagine that they were engaged exclusively in such business. One often hears the generalization that schooners were not satisfactory for deepwater transoceanic voyages but there is plenty of specific evidence to disprove it. It cannot be denied that certain large schooners had a bad time of it on deepwater passages but the difficulty must be attributed more to the particular type and size of schooner than to all fore-and-afters.

From the outset, schooners often made long voyages to distant ports in Europe and the Far East. The three-masters often found their way to Europe, Africa, and South America, as did their larger successors on occasion, while several doubled Cape Horn to Australia. An example of such deepwater activity is reflected in the logbooks of the three-masted schooner *Island City,* which was built at East Boston in 1871. On her maiden voyage she went to Philadelphia, where she loaded petroleum for Alexandria, Egypt. She was thirty-three days to Gibraltar, and nineteen days later anchored at her destination. Proceeding to Trapani, Sicily, she loaded a part cargo of salt and completed her lading at Messina with wines, nuts, oranges, lemons and sulfur. She was forty-three days to Boston. After a ten-months' interlude of coasting which ended in March 1873, she loaded cotton at Galveston for Bremen, Germany. From there she went to Gothenburg and loaded iron for Boston. Her next voyage was from New York to Genoa with oil, returning from Catania and Messina. After a few more coasting voyages, the schooner loader lumber at Pensacola for Buenos Aires. Returning home, she loaded a cargo of rifles, bullets, cartridges, shells, pistols, and bayonets at New Haven, finally delivering these warlike stores to the Sultan's representative at Constantinople. Her next call was at Taganrog, a Russian port on the Sea of Azov, where she loaded linseed for Falmouth, England. She then visited Hull and Shields, Palermo and Messina, thence to Boston with a stop at Bermuda for repairs. In May 1876, she was back in New Haven for another cargo of munitions for Constantinople. At Scale Nova in Asia Minor she loaded a cargo of licorice for New York. The end of 1876 found *Island City* outward bound from New York with case oil for Melbourne. She rounded Cape Horn and arrived at Melbourne after a passage of 100 days. Williamstown and Newcastle, New South Wales, were next visited before returning home. After voyages to Oporto, Portugal, and Cadiz, Spain, the schooner went back to coasting and finally was operated as a regular packet between Baltimore and Savannah.[7]

The three-master *George V. Jordan* was another fore-and-aft deepwaterman. She was somewhat larger than *Island City* registering nearly 700 tons and was built in 1874 at Kennebunk. On at least two occasions she made voyages lasting two years before returning home. These took her to Australia, China, South Africa, Ceylon, and our own Pacific coast. She spent so much time offshore that she carried a single yard on her foremast to permit her to set a square foresail in the trade winds.[8]

Quite a different picture is gained from the letters of Captain F. W. Patten, who took the five-masted steel schooner *Kineo* to Manila and Australia in 1905-1906.[9] From Manila he reported to his owners that often even when the wind was fair he was obliged to lower his sails because the seas caused the vessel to roll and to slat her sails so badly as to break the gaffs repeatedly.

> Another thing against the schooner is the necessity of reducing sail in latitudes where gales are to be expected . . . . the sails have to be reefed in time or they cannot be handled with the heavy water washing across the decks. I also expected to be able to do without steam after getting off shore but we have had so many light winds and heavy swell at the same time, sometimes hoisting lower sails several times a day, that water has been another cause for worry. A vessel of this kind should have a salt water boiler for these trips.

On his return to Philadelphia with sugar from Hawaii after a passage of 205 days, Captain Patten reported:

The seas were heavy and the ship has been dismantled five different times.  Sails gone and unable to make repairs for weeks at a time owing to the fact of the seas making such breach right over the ship.  To make matters worse the tubes in our boiler gave out and everything had to be done by hand with no means aboard for heaving.  The wear and tear has been something enormous.

The steam power so badly missed on *Kineo's* voyage was a necessary feature of the large schooners.  As the size of schooners got beyond five hundred tons, the sails and gear aboard became heavy and unwieldly.  In bad weather the big sails became very hard to handle with the small crews that were characteristic of schooners.  Not until 1879, however, was steam power introduced on schooners, and even after that date, many vessels remained hand-pullers, aboard which all sail handling and anchor weighing was done by "main strength and perspiration."

It was on *Charles A. Briggs*, a 758-ton three-master built at Bath, Maine, in 1879 that a steam windlass was first installed for the purpose of hoisting the heavy sails, getting up the anchor, pumping the bilges, and discharging cargo.  Some idea of the practical advantage that steam offered over the old system is to be gained from the following comparison.  Among the first schooners to have a steam hoisting engine was *Josie R. Burt*, a 760-ton three-master built at Bath in 1882.  On one occasion she was in company with *Zaccheus Sherman*, a hand-puller of similar size, both anchored awaiting a favorable slant of the wind.  When the wind shifted, *Burt* hauled her anchor and thirty fathoms of chain and had everything set in thirty minutes.  On the other hand, *Sherman* took "half a day" to get under way and make all sail, by which time *Burt* was long since gone.[10]

The following comments about an American schooner as seen through English eyes provide a fascinating vignette.  The encounter described occurred in 1889 in the St. Mary's River on the border between Florida and Georgia.

I haven't told you that a neighbor arrived a few days ago, a handsome 'down east' schooner (three masted) called the *Susie P. Oliver*.  Please note the initial letter, without which an American name would be incomplete.  Almost all American vessels are named after some individual (an abominably tasteless fashion), and every name must of necessity include the initial, as Joel F. Hopkins, Amanda K. Jones.  They are great institutions, these same schooners, for owing to their simplicity of rig, they can sail a vessel of 900 tons capacity with eight hands all told. They sail well, shift without ballast, use but little gear, and rarely exceed thirteen feet in draught. Perhaps the first thing that strikes a stranger's eyes is their enormous beam. This schooner alongside of us is of much less tonnage than the *Mertola* but her beam is thirty-five feet, the *Mertola*'s being twenty-nine feet. One would think that so much breadth with so little depth would make them very skittish in a seaway, and be terribly severe upon the masts, but they seem to get along all right, and undoubtedly sail like foam balls. Their cabin accommodations make me quite envious. Imagine, my sea-faring friends, a skipper having a private sitting-room, ten feet by ten feet, with spare side rooms off it; a bedroom abaft, ten feet by seven feet; large bathroom and companion way—all in his own quarters; while on the fore side of his bulkhead is a cabin, ten by twelve; with mates' berths, pantry, steward's room, etc. on each side. This, my dear British shipowner, is the accommodation given to a coasting skipper; while his wages, if monthly, run from £20 upwards; if he sails his ship on shares, often much more than this. The skipper of the *Susie* proves to be a great acquisition. He is an elderly individual, of the decided 'down east' pattern so familiar to us through the pages of Oliver Wendell Holmes, with a lean, leathery visage, as impassive as the back of a ledger—an illustration which promptly brings me up to my bearings by 'not to judge a book from its cover.' As it turns out, this same solemn-visaged, slow-of-speech, old Yankee salt is as full of fun as a kitten and as tender hearted as a child.[11]

The schooner described was a vessel of 272 tons, built at Bucksport, Maine, in 1882. That she must have been a stout vessel is suggested by the fact that in 1919 she was sold to French interests and renamed *Somme*. *Mertola* was a barque of 393 tons register, built in Nova Scotia for London owners in 1866.

The largest three-masted schooner ever built was *Bradford C. French*, which was launched from David Clark's Kennebunkport yard in 1884. She was a powerful vessel of 920 tons with necessarily large and heavy sails. She was built for the coal trade and hailed originally from Taunton, Massachusetts, where a great many of the early coal schooners were owned. Her last master, Captain

O. R. Farrell, recalls that when he took command of *French* in 1915 she was an old, strained and weakened vessel.

> We towed out of Boston in a light fair wind and as we went down the harbor we commenced to set sail. Finally we set the spanker, a real brute of a sail it was, too, with double sheets. Outside there was a little swell running and she'd roll with it. When she did, that whoppin' big spanker would fetch up first one way and then the other, and the whole stern of that schooner would twist with it. Just like one of them Cuban rhumba dancers. I hollered to the mate, 'Haul that thing down before she tears the stern off'n her.' We went down to Newport News in four days and we never did set that spanker.[12]

By 1880 the three-masters, too, were reaching their practical limit in size, and in the same year that steam power was introduced to the schooner fleet, two other significant events occurred: the steamer *Weybosset* was converted to sail and equipped with four masts. Also, the firm of Goss & Sawyer at Bath commenced construction of a large schooner, which, when launched in 1880, became *William L. White,* the first four-masted schooner built as such.

Henry Hall's government report on the shipbuilding industry in 1880 makes this observation about the four-masted *White*, then brand new:

> The hull of the vessel is large enough for a Californian. She is 205 feet long on deck, 40 feet beam, and 17 feet deep in the hold, being 309 feet in length from the end of the jibboom to the end of the spanker boom. She registers 996 tons and is able to carry 1450 tons of anthracite coal. ....To have fitted her with three masts would have required such large lower sails that the strain upon the masts would have been destructive, and she was therefore furnished with four, the after spar being called the spanker mast. This divided her 5,017 yards of canvas into smaller sails and made her a good schooner, sailing well, easily handled, and requiring a crew of only five men before the mast, besides her two mates and captain.[13]

Interestingly enough, the second four-master was a much smaller vessel of only 496 tons. This was *Francis C. Yarnall*, which was built at Wilmington, Delaware, in 1881. Thereafter the vessels got larger year by year and hull by hull. *Elliott B. Church*, built at Bath in 1882, was the first to exceed 1,000 tons. *Augustus Hunt*, launched later the same year at Bath, was of 1,200 tons.

While the three-masters continued to be built in large numbers and found ready employment serving smaller ports inaccessible to large vessels of greater draft, the four-masters were built in ever increasing numbers. In 1890, no less than forty-one four-masted schooners were launched, the largest number to be set afloat in a single year. Thirty-two were launched in 1891. Not until World War I were four-masters produced again in such numbers. Thirty-one were launched in 1917, and thirty-nine in each of the two following years. When the last four-master was built in 1921, some 459 such vessels had been built during the 41-year period.

The same forces which produced the four-master in 1880 led in turn to the experiment of five masts. In 1888, Captain Cornelius Davis of Somerset, Massachusetts, made arrangements to have a large schooner built at Waldoboro, Maine. The designer, Albert Winslow of Taunton, decided to try a five-masted rig, thereby reducing the size of the sails. This became the 1,764-ton *Governor Ames*. Launched on 1 December 1888, she was a tremendously strong vessel and a smart sailer. She was the only five-master to be equipped with a centerboard. She had the misfortune to be totally dismasted on her maiden voyage due to the stretching of the rigging in a severe blow, and this saddled the vessel with a $20,000 repair bill before she had earned a nickel.

It may be mentioned parenthetically that before many years had passed the use of lanyards and deadeyes to set up the shrouds and backstays was abandoned and heavy turnbuckles became the order of the day. Eventually, wire rope came into use for the standing rigging and the danger of stretching rigging which cost *Governor Ames* so dearly became only an unpleasant memory.

*Governor Ames* suffered from an undeserved reputation as a failure because of the heavy financial handicap that beset her and the business depression which prevailed during the Nineties. In an effort to recoup her losses, she went round the Horn to the Pacific coast, where she was employed for four years during which she made a voyage to Australia. Finally she returned East and re-entered the coal trade, continuing until 1910, when she was lost by stranding on the North Carolina coast with heavy loss of life.

Ten years passed after *Governor Ames* was launched before another five-master was built. Meanwhile four-masters had increased in size to 2,000 tons, and that was the practical limit. The largest four-master was *Frank A. Palmer*, 2,015 tons, built at Bath by N. T. Palmer in 1897. The following year the 2,400-ton five-master *Nathaniel T. Palmer* was launched at Bath, and in 1899 the slightly larger *John B. Prescott* was built at Camden, Maine. The popularity of five-masters now grew rapidly, and ultimately a total of fifty-six of this rig was built — all but four of them in Maine. The last five-master was *Edna Hoyt*, 1,512 tons, built at Thomaston, Maine, in 1920. She continued in operation until November 1937, when, while bound from Wales to Venezuela with patent fuel, she was towed into Lisbon in a leaking and seriously damaged condition after a severe buffeting in the Bay of Biscay.

The year 1900 saw the construction at Camden, Maine, of the first six-master, *George W. Wells*. Scarcely two months later, the Bath shipyard of Percy & Small launched the second six-master, *Eleanor A. Percy*. At nearly 3,500 tons she was some 300 tons larger than *Wells*. There were ten of these giants built between 1900 and 1909. One of them was of steel construction and built at the Fore River shipyard at Quincy, Massachusetts. Of the nine wooden six-masters, all were built in Maine, seven of them by Percy & Small at Bath. The last and greatest was *Wyoming*, one of the largest wooden sailing vessels of any rig ever built. She registered 3,730 tons and could carry 6,000 tons of coal. She was lost with all hands in 1924 while bound from Norfolk to St. John, New Brunswick, with coal. She anchored off Chatham during a northeast gale, and in the violence of her pitching she apparently struck bottom, opened up and sank.

On one occasion *Wyoming* loaded 6,004 tons of coal at Newport News for Boston. Captain Kreger in *Edward J. Lawrence* fancied it would be quite a stunt to carry one more ton than *Wyoming*, so he had the trimmers pack her full and loaded her as deeply as he dared. When he got his bill of lading it showed that 6,001 tons had been put aboard. The schooner had so little residual buoyancy that her passage to Boston was both unpleasant and dangerous. Nobody doubted thereafter that *Wyoming* was the larger carrier, certainly not Captain Kreger.[14]

It was in *Wyoming* that the building of wooden schooners reached its highest point of development. Yet one of Maine's outstanding master shipbuilders, John J. Wardwell, who designed and built many large schooners including *George W. Wells,* has declared, "Six-masters were not practical. They were too long for wooden construction."[15]

The huge schooners, particularly the six-masters, had inherent weaknesses due to their great length which taxed to the utmost the ingenuity of their builders. In these vessels the ratio of length to beam was six and one-half to one, whereas the clippers of fifty years before had a ratio of five and one-half to one. While they were as long as the square-riggers, they did not have the corresponding depth of hold. They could not have operated in the onshore trades for which they were intended had they been deeper. They drew every foot of water that was available to them as it was, and at low tide usually grounded out at the dock. This of course strained the hulls unmercifully.

The design of the schooners was such that with a full midsection of great buoyancy and heavily laden ends of relatively little buoyancy, there was a powerful tendency for the ends to drop. When this occurred the vessel was described as being *hogged.* In an only partially successful effort to overcome this weakness, the vessels were constructed with keelson and 'sister keelsons of tremendous depth. Six tiers of 15x15 timber formed the keelson with 'sister keelsons on either side of three or four tiers of similar stuff. This provided a pretty rugged backbone when fastened through the floor timbers and keel. Many of the largest schooners were strapped; that is to say, a diagonal network of heavy iron straps was put in flush to the surface of the frame under the planking and securely fastened to the frame, extending from the level of the deck to the turn of the bilges. All the great schooners and most of the lesser ones were built with much more sheer than had been customary with the earlier square-riggers. The turned-up bows and stern were not only pleasing to the eye but were calculated to conceal some of the tendency of the ends of the vessel to drop. The great sheer also served to keep the poop and forecastle relatively dry when the vessel was deep-laden.

The desire to overcome the weaknesses of large wooden hulls and the limitations which these imposed led to experiments in steel schooner construction. Among these were the five-masted *Kineo* built at Bath in 1903 by A. Sewall & Co., the six-masted *William L. Douglas* and the unique seven-masted *Thomas W. Lawson*, both built at Quincy, Massachusetts, in 1902.

No discussion of large schooners can ignore the famous *Lawson* however atypical she may have been. Designed by B. B. Crowninshield, as was *Douglas*, she was an enormously powerful vessel. She measured 395 feet overall, with a fifty-foot beam, and a depth of thirty-two feet. Fully loaded with 9,200 tons of coal, she drew twenty-nine feet, ten inches. She had seven steel masts, the foremast being thirty-three inches in diameter. Equipped with ballast tanks in her double bottom and fore and aft peak tanks, she carried 1,069 tons of water ballast in which condition she drew twelve feet.

Her designer states that *Lawson* handled well when loaded but required depths of water that were not always easily found on the routes she was obliged to travel. Light, she handled satisfactorily with a leading wind but tacking in moderate weather was often difficult and sometimes impossible.

When she could be no longer operated profitably in the coal trade, she was converted to a tanker by the division of her hull into fourteen tanks. In November 1907, she loaded nearly two and one-half million gallons of lubricating oil and sailed from Marcus Hook for England. After a tempestuous passage of six weeks, she anchored in the open sea off the Scilly Isles. A heavy gale parted both her chains and she drove ashore in the middle of the night. Three men were picked up, but one of them died shortly after getting ashore. Only Captain Dow and Engineer Rowe survived the disaster.[16]

Masters in the coal trade commonly sailed on the basis of $50 per month plus five per cent of the gross freight. In other words, they accepted a nominal salary of $50 a month but their true income would be a reflection of their enterprise and seamanship in making as many round trips to the coal ports as might be possible. The Master also customarily owned an interest in the vessel, generally at least one sixty-fourth share, and consequently participated further in the vessel's earnings. The other shares were held by a large and heterogeneous group often including many from midwestern states, as well as New England home town folks and city merchants.

The Masters of the large schooners were remarkable seamen and navigators. It was no easy task to handle a big schooner along the crowded waters of the Atlantic coast, working through Vineyard Sound and over Nantucket Shoals with the risks of stranding ever threatening. The usual courses of the schooners cut across the regular routes of the transatlantic and West Indies steamships, and at night and in thick weather the schooners were often in danger of collision with steamers whose officers either misjudged the course and speed of the sailing vessel or failed altogether to see her. The sailing vessel Masters seemed to develop an intuitive faculty in conning their vessels safely through the shoals and bars about Cape Cod. They knew intimately the influences on their vessels of the currents, tide rips, wind and weather. Practically all of them started their careers before the mast in small coasters, becoming Mate as their skill and maturity developed. When they had saved enough to buy a Master's share in a small vessel, they became shipmasters and improved themselves with larger vessels as their skill, industry, and circumstances permitted.

The prevailing winds along the shore are southwesterly, so that the southward passage from New England ports was a beat to windward, while the return trip usually enjoyed a favorable wind. When bound South from Boston, the schooner Master would lay his course about southeast past Cape Cod and out what is known as the South Channel, that unmarked stretch of water between Nantucket Shoals and Georges Bank. In the neighborhood of Nantucket Shoals lightship he would come about onto the port tack and take a long leg inshore along the southerly shore of Long Island until he got well up under the New Jersey coast. From there he would continue southward in shorter tacks, customarily standing offshore on a long tack during the day and coming in under the New Jersey or Virginia shore in the evening to take advantage of the night breeze, which was likely to blow more directly offshore and thus enable the schooner to make a more southerly course down the coast. Sometimes the wind would haul directly in the eye of the schooner's course. When this happened, rather than spend their time beating back and forth for negligible gains, many Masters preferred to anchor right were they were, ten or fifteen miles at sea, and wait for a more favorable slant.

On the other hand, a big five or six-master might get away from Portland or Boston in the teeth of a northwesterly gale. With such a chance, flying light with the wind on her quarter, a big schooner made great time. What might normally take a week or two could be accomplished in a matter of hours. Running before a northwester, the six-master *Ruth E. Merrill* once ran to Norfolk from Portland in forty-five hours, averaging thirteen knots or somewhat better than the speed of a coastwise freight steamer of that time. *George W. Wells* is said to have made a passage from Boston to Cape Henry in thirty-nine hours. Sometimes, however, these winter northwesters led to disaster and vessels were occasionally blown so far offshore that they had considerable difficulty clawing their way back when they finally reached the latitude of Cape Henry. It was not altogether uncommon for a schooner to turn up weeks later at Bermuda with sails blown away, or even in Puerto Rico, St. Thomas, or some other West Indies port.

The trip north was generally a fair run before the prevailing wind. Usually the course was direct from Hampton Roads up the coast to the Vineyard lightship at the entrance to Vineyard Sound. From that point the course lay up Vineyard Sound past Vineyard Haven and through the channel between the bars and shoals of Nantucket Sound until the vessel finally ran out into the Atlantic again past Monomoy at the elbow of Cape Cod. There the course turned abruptly northward along the Cape until at Highland Light the course was laid directly for Boston or Portland.

Occasionally northeast gales interrupted the normally fair northward passage. This would produce a great congregation of vessels at Vineyard Haven, all waiting for a favorable opportunity to get around Cape Cod. During such a spell a week might elapse without a single coal schooner arriving at either Portland or Boston. Finally, when the wind hauled to the south'ard, perhaps fifteen or twenty or more schooners might report at the coal docks in Boston between eight o'clock and noon so that the last to arrive, though only a few hours behind the others, might have to wait a couple of weeks to get a place to unload.[17]

The following description of part of an 1897 trip from Hampton Roads to Portland in the four-master *Sarah C. Ropes* captures much of the drama that was a common ingredient in coasting passages.

Finally the heft of the storm hit us and I have never seen anything so terrifying. The entire sea was knocked flat, flat as a table top and not a wave could raise its head. They were sheared off and sent flying through the air like huge white table cloths torn off a clothes line by a tornado, turning over and over as they scurried by to leeward. The ship went over on her side with a crash of dishes in the pantry and the cabin furniture tumbling about below. She didn't quite go over on her beam ends but she thrust her entire lee rail and bulwarks under and the water was up to the hatch coamings on the poop. I clung to the spanker boom gasping for breath as it was taken clean out of me even with my face turned to leeward. The spume and spindrift lashed the back of my neck, hurting like hailstones. I dared not turn my face to windward. Overhead the wind screamed and shrieked in the rigging as if all the devils in Hell had let loose.

With the passing of the blast the wind moderated and the sea rose again. We paid off and scudded before it toward the smoother water of Vineyard Sound. After passing Gay Head we kept right on bowling down the Sound before a spanking breeze. We were headed for Pollock Rip Slue, at the elbow of Cape Cod, hoping to reach it before night and the turn of the tide, which would enable us to get through. It is a nasty spot. There is a narrow channel of deep water with shoals on either hand and a strong tide rip. It requires a sharp turn to get through.

There was a tremendous swell running outside and some doubt of there being enough water under our keel, deeply laden as we were. But valuable time had been lost. Topsails were crowded on until just before we reached the Slue when they were doused to enable a quick gybe over if necessary in paying off for the turn. We managed without having to gybe but directly afterward we hit bottom in the let down between the swells and I thought the masts would come out of her. Everyone on deck danced like monkeys on a hot stove. I still have a vision of Captain Kreger executing his caper with his behind wiggling like a rabbit's and decidedly comical. But I had no stomach for laughter just then. We hit bottom three times between swells before getting through. Fortunately it was all sand and no rocks so no apparent damage was done.[18]

171

Several of the bigger fleets of schooners retained a reporter, generally a retired mariner, at Vineyard Haven whose duty it was to telegraph the managing owners or agents at Boston or Portland whenever one of their vessels passed the Vineyard eastward bound. Thus forewarned, the agent could arrange for a tug to meet the schooner and tow her into port without delay on the following day and make arrangements also for prompt discharge of the cargo.[19]

Under the most favorable circumstances it was possible for a schooner to make a round voyage in the coal trade in a couple of weeks. *Eleanor A. Percy* went from Boston to Newport News, and returned thirteen days later with 5,500 tons of coal. Six years later the four-master *Frontenac* made the same trip in nine days. The average time for such a round trip was about three weeks—a week going South, a week getting loaded, and a week returning. Eleven to fourteen round trips a year was good going.[20]

All good things must come to an end, and, except for the brief but spectacular burst of construction produced by the high freight rates of World War I, the end of great schooner construction came just prior to 1910. Many shipyards in Massachusetts and New York had failed or closed down during the business stagnation of the 1890's but this had merely given the Maine yards more to do. Soon, however, even their long-held advantage of cheap labor was not enough to overcome the trend of rising costs. All the ship timber, once so plentiful, had to be transported great distances. Oak frames were cut in North Carolina or wherever good stands of oak could be located. All the hard pine came from southern ports. Hackmatack knees were shipped in from Nova Scotia. Masts were shipped round or brought by railroad from the Oregon pine forests. Shipbuilding costs rose from $40 per ton average in 1900 to $52 per ton in 1907.[21]

Ironically, the very forces which produced the big schooners now turned to destroy them. The quantities of coal demanded at New England ports exceeded the ability of wooden sailing vessels to supply. Schooners could not guarantee regularity of delivery and steamers could. When three large steam colliers were built and put on the Norfolk-New England run in 1907, the handwriting was on the wall in large letters. Many ocean-going towboats were employed hauling long strings of barges bringing coal from Hampton

Roads. Many of the barges were old sailing vessel hulls with all but the lower masts removed, on which a few yards of canvas were set to steady the barge and help the tow. Morse, the Bath shipbuilder, commenced to build big barges especially for this trade.

Though practically no new vessels were built between 1909 and 1915, the schooner fleet struggled on in a losing battle for economic survival. Many of those that were left afloat when freight rates skyrocketed in World War I made a killing. They were sold and resold at several times their cost and sent across the Atlantic with war supplies. Some fell prey to U-boats; some foundered on the way over; it often made little difference to the owners what happened to the vessel as they had a huge prepaid freight in hand.

The story of the wartime schooner fleet, including a host of new vessels that were produced between 1915 and 1921 is a fascinating one and deserves the attention of some historian. The boom was largely synthetic in character and while the fortunate early ones reaped a harvest of gold, more were unfortunately too late and paid no return at all. A few four-masters lived long enough to die in World War II.

In a scholarly work entitled *American Maritime Industries* and published by the Harvard University Press in 1941, the author, John Hutchins, has written: "The great schooner was the last technical achievement of the builders of the wooden ships. Notable advances were made in model and rig, but particularly the latter. These made the American great schooner the most weatherly and economical sailing vessel in the world."

1   W. J. L. Parker, *The Great Coal Schooners of New England* (Mystic, Conn.: The Marine Historical Association, Inc., 1948), p. 14.
2   W. H. Rowe, *The Maritime History of Maine* (New York: W. W. Norton & Co., 1948), pp. 259-262.
3   G. S. Wasson, *Sailing Days on the Penobscot* (Salem: Marine Research Society, 1932).
4   W. J. L. Parker, op. cit., pp. 16-19.

5   C. C. Cutler, *Queens of the Western Ocean* (Annapolis, Md.: U. S. Naval Institute, 1961), p. 551.

6   W. J. L. Parker, op. cit., p. 30.

7   *Baltimore Sun*, 25 January 1890; Note furnished by W. J. L. Parker.

8   C. S. Morgan, *Shipbuilding on the Kennebec* (Kennebunkport, Me.: Kennebunkport Historical Society, 1952), pp. 20-22.

9   M. W. Hennessy, *Sewall Ships of Steel* (Augusta, Me.: Kennebec Journal Press, 1937), pp. 366, 371.

10  W. J. L. Parker, op. cit. p. 35.

11  A. J. Green, *Jottings From a Cruise* (Seattle: Kelly Printing Co., 1944), pp. 145-147.

12  C. S. Morgan, op. cit., p. 27.

13  H. Hall, *Report on the Shipbuilding Industry in the United States* (Washington: Tenth U. S. Census, 1880).

14  H. G. Foss, unpublished memorandum.

15  H. Buxton, *Assignment Down East* (Brattleboro, Vt.: Stephen Daye Press, 1938), p. 191.

16  B. B. Crowinshield, *Fore and Afters* (Boston: Houghton Mifflin Co., 1940) pp. 54-56.

17  R. E. Peabody, unpublished manuscript.

18  W. S. Laurence, *Coasting Passage* (Arlington, Mass.: C. S. Morgan, 1949) pp. 31-32.

19  W. J. L. Parker, op. cit. p. 55.

20  W. J. L. Parker, ibid., p. 57.

21  W. J. L. Parker, ibid., p. 47.

# *About The Big Coasters*

## JOHN T. ROWLAND

IT SEEMS THAT MOST YACHTSMEN FEEL A SORT OF PITYING CONTEMPT for coasters. I, personally, do not think I've ever heard a kind word said for one, although the rummest little "crate" that fishes on Georges is generally regarded nowadays with reverent awe. The reason is not far to seek: it lies in the easy, graceful lines of the fisherman as contrasted with the full and heavy ones of the coaster.

What was it the Romans called their freighters? "Round ships," I think it was, in distinction to the *naves longae* which were the scout cruisers and destroyers of those oar-loving days. I remember studying the picture of a bowl-shaped merchantman in my *Commentaries* and wondering how those ancient seafarers managed to make voyages to the Cassiterides (which we nowadays call the Scilly Isles) and come back safe through the Pillars of Hercules loaded to their ports with ore. They were bulk cargo ships, just as our big coasters are principally today. Cedar from Lebanon, tin from Britain, grain from Egypt—it would be easy to match their ladings with those borne by our own four-masted schooners; and in both cases the designers doubtless came by similar courses to the same conclusion, namely, that a freighter is useless unless she can carry a load. So the easy lines of the "long ship" were abandoned in favor of a greater capacity of hold, just as the fine entrance of

Reprinted from *Yachting* for March 1927 by permission of the author and Yachting Publishing Corporation.

175

the clipper has been sacrificed to give a form which may compete economically with steam.

But here is the thing to remark: in each case the loss in handiness is put up to the master to overcome. It does not seem much of a feat, after all, to handle a fine, smart little Gloucester schooner with a husky crew of men; one would be rather "wooden" not to come out where he desired. But to go to sea in a great hulk drawing 17 feet of water and loaded with 1500 tons of dead weight, having no other power than that of her sails and only the help of a donkey engine and a few green hands to work those, to be hampered moreover by rotten canvas and old gear, and yet to make a voyage to Trinidad or the River Plate and back in the space of a few months without loss—there you have something that still calls for seamanship of the old-fashioned sort. And the same holds good, perhaps more so, of vessels that go "down east" in midwinter—to Boston, Portland, St. John, even to Nova Scotia and Newfoundland, loaded to the deck with coal. It is easy to scoff, but next time you speed past some big lump of a four-master that behaves as though rooted to bottom just stop and think where she may have been.

Perhaps I have been too ready to accept the slurs. The fact is that one of these big Yankee schooners is a masterpiece in her way. It happens that her way differs somewhat from that of the fish killers, but it is no less worthy of honor for that. The conditions her design must fulfill are probably the most difficult by which a naval architect has ever been confronted, and the way in which our down-east shipwrights managed to harmonize seeming contradictions is rather wonderful when you come to study it a bit.

It was the failure of the square-riggers to compete with steam that led enterprising builders to consider the possibilities of the fore-and-aft rig, which hitherto had only been used for small vessels. The greater difficulty with the clippers was their enormous crews, which became prohibitive when wages soared. When the clippers passed, the crews of the square-rigged cargo carriers were cut to the minimum possible. To reduce these further without decreasing the vessels' size, and at the same time turn out a ship which could make coasting voyages against contrary winds; to produce a sturdy flat-floored hull that would take no damage by beaching on the Fundy flats and yet could work to windward in a Hatteras gale, one which would be deep enough to ride out a blow at sea, yet able to ascend the shallow southern rivers, and finally to produce a sailing vessel on a large scale which, in spite of the conditions mentioned, could make a long deep water voyage in fair time when occasion demanded—there was a proposition to turn a designer's hair grey.

I may be getting ahead of myself, but right here I must tell you how well it has been answered by citing the case of a particular ship that I know. She is a four-masted schooner of 1400 tons dead-weight capacity (about 200 feet long o.a.) and she carries a complement of only nine people, all told. She has made a voyage from Axim, on the West Coast of Africa, to Boston in 60 days with a full cargo of mahogany logs; from Blue Hill, Maine to Trinidad in about three weeks with three million barrel staves in her hold and on deck; from Trinidad to Mobile in 15 days with asphalt; and from Brunswick, Georgia, to New York in 11 days in midwinter with 612 ninety-foot sticks of piling on board. I have known her to beat into a narrow harbor in the West Indies and berth herself where there was no tug to help; I have seen her perched high and dry beside a Fundy dock with 1250 tons of rock in her hold, and I have known her to do her 10 knots, loaded, for three days running before an easterly gale, although that is her worst point of sailing. And yet yachtsmen have the cheek to call such vessels old tubs!

For one who has been fond of navigating great waters in small yachts the big fore-and-after holds a paradoxical charm, because she is the nearest thing to a single-hander that exists above 30 feet in length. Far fetched this may sound, yet it is, in my experience, literally true.

Several summers ago I made a run in one which carried no sailors and no mate (although a few country lads and myself were down on articles) and in which the skipper and donkey-engineer were the only qualified people. Yet I made out well enough by imagining that I was sailing an oversized sloop, and the boys were all right when they had learned the obvious difference between a halliard and a sheet: all they ever did was to lead along the rope indicated to the winch and hold a turn on the nigger-head while the donkeyman gave her the steam. This latter was an artist at his trade; he knew not only to a hair how high each sail should go and how flat the huge fore-and-afters would stand, but just how much strain it was safe to put on a down-haul when dousing sail in a squall. The skipper was unusually fortunate in having such an able winchman. For the winch itself is practically the crew of such a vessel, with the few hands as mere accessories to make the necessary mechanical connection between it and the sails. With that their usefulness ceases: nearly everything that partakes of intelligent effort is done by the skipper himself. Even to mending sails.

Under such conditions it is not strange that a unique technique has been developed. The old-style sail-handling depended altogether upon men; blow high or blow low Jack ran aloft and smothered the struggling canvas by sheer beef and guts, thereby frequently saving the day despite bad judgment, indifference or bravado on the part of his superiors. The schooner skipper has no such last resort. A donkey engine cannot hand or reef a sail, so the skipper well knows that unless he lowers them in time no power but God Almighty's will get the great rhomboids down—and when He does it there is not apt to be much left but shreds. Accordingly the master of a modern coaster has to be ever on the alert and thinking several hours ahead. If the sea is getting up and the sky looks hard and windy he has the alternative of shortening sail before he needs to, or of hanging on and taking a chance on having his canvas blown away. The same thing applies, naturally, to whether he shall run or heave-to, and the result is that in no other type of ship are weather wisdom and real judgment such important factors. Give me a down-east coaster skipper every time for a man who knows his stuff. The fish killers don't belong in the same class.

I knew a master who sailed a big four-sticker all through the West Indies discharging piecemeal a cargo of thirty-thousand ten-gallon cases of kerosene. He sailed from Port Arthur, on the west side of the Gulf, in the middle of August. The winds were light and it would have been impossible to get through the Yucatan channel against the strong current setting north. The "trades" in the Carribbean would also have been ahead. Accordingly he stood to the eastward and went out through the Straits of Florida with the Gulf Stream. Holding this with a fair wind for several days he made good time to about 30° N., where he swung her off and ran east again until Bermuda bore north. Then he shaped a course to the southeast and after a week or more of "light airs and variable" drew into the edge of the northeast trade winds. He had now a sure source of power, but even so care was needed not to let the vessel sag off, for had she done so there would have been no way to get back except by swinging clear round the circle a second time.

Going south he met a hurricane, but brought the wind on his quarter and ran out of it without losing any sails. He stood well to windward of his destination and when at last the island of Martinique was under his lee he ran down for it and made his first port of call. Having discharged there the allotted portion of his cargo, he ran down wind through the whole chain of the Antilles, visiting each of his ports in turn and docking the vessel without the aid of a tug. Samana Bay, in San Domingo, gave him a little trouble as the waters are treacherous and poorly charted and he had to beat out of it with the trades in his teeth; but he gained the Mona Passage at last and was able to make a a fair wind.

This voyage would have been one to write home about had you made it in a smart schooner yacht, yet this man did it with a ship which during the first part was loaded to 17 feet, and towards the end was so light that she would not tack and it was necessary to lower the spanker each time to wear her around. But to her skipper it was part of the day's work, tedious and vexatious in part but not remarkable in any other respect. The only thing he complained of was the time wasted in port due to the worthlessness of native stevedores. And it is to be noted that while this ship might have driven a fisherman crazy she was nevertheless able to "deliver the goods," handled by a master who had the requisite knowledge and skill. She carried 1400 tons of freight and had a crew of master, mate, winchman, cook and four colored sailors—about what you might need on a 70-foot schooner yacht. Her spanker alone would make a whole suit of sails for such a craft.

You may always notice a fine pair of "mud-hooks" on the bows, and it is not for ornament that the coasting skipper has ground tackle of the best. Where the old school windjammer used to claw offshore to meet a gale the big coaster very often hunts the beach and plants his two anchors, backed by a long scope of chain. There are several good reasons for this departure from standard seamanship. In the first place the most severe and longest gales are from the north and west, from which the Atlantic coast in most parts offers a lee. Also, the bottom is shelving and the vessels are so big that they can anchor a dozen miles from the beach and not feel the sea if the wind is off the land. But even when caught on a dead lee shore like Cape Cod in an easterly gale they will often anchor and ride it out. This is one reason for the high clipper bows and raking nose poles. A square-rigger could not do it owing to the tremendous wind resistance of her spars aloft. If, however, she is caught far at sea your coaster will heave-to under a bit of storm sail — usually a reefed main or a trysail on one of the after masts — and lie as comfortably as any other ship.

It is not that she is forced to anchor off the beach, but that her ability to do so successfully is a great advantage which most large sailing ships do not possess. She can thus always hold what she has gained. It is especially valuable on long coasting voyages where good harbors are few and the water is shallow, as off the Carolinas, with promontories like Hatteras to pass.

I shall never forget my surprise the first time I helped get a big four-master underway. Instead of half a day it took less than a half hour to hoist the four big lower sails. No jigs or watch-tackles to sweat up — the "iron sailor" up forward certainly made for simplicity of gear. He also hove up the anchor at a merry clip. Leaving me at the wheel, the skipper ran forward to supervise hoisting the jibs. When these were set and the ship began to pay off I put my helm hard down to meet her; but I might as well have stuck out an oar over the stern. Off she swung, further and further, until her raking jibboom pointed for the tree-tops not many hundred yards away. At last, with a fresh breeze over her quarter, the straining canvas overcame the tremendous inertia of her deep laden hull and she began to move, with a mound of water against her lee side and whirlpools in her wake. Slowly then she rounded up towards the wind; I put my helm hard up and suc-ceeded in catching her before she went about. It took her a good five minutes to gather way, but once she had done so she balanced as nicely as a yacht. Her speed in a nice fresh breeze was about seven knots — a trifle better than that of the aver-age small tramp.

One curious thing I noticed quite early in this voyage was that there seemed to be a critical point in the wind's force below which she would scarcely move at all. This was the point at which whitecaps began to appear, and it was astonishing to see how rapidly her speed increased once this point was passed. With a whole sail breeze of twenty knots she would do a good eight, on the wind, and perhaps nine with a quartering sea. She was so stiff and the masts were so heavily stayed that the only thing we had to look out for was our canvas and lighter spars. At about thirty knots topsails would be clewed up, and when it blew a moderate gale the foresail would be lowered (it was rotten and old) and the spanker double reefed to balance. We had to watch our canvas more carefully when running off than close hauled, owing to the fact that in the latter instance the sails spilled the wind. Our great bugaboo was leeway, which lessened as the ship's speed increased, but the skipper was always careful to note the course made good.

This leeway puzzled me more than a little, since the vessel was wall sided for two-thirds of her length and drew 17 feet. It seemed as though that should have given sufficient lateral resistance to hold her, but it did not. She was almost flat underneath and had a straight keel about two feet deep. The skipper subsequently added a false keel or shoe only six inches deep, and I have been told that that trifling addition reduced her leeway by half. Apparently it is the lateral plane in dead water that counts.

When we tacked the only thing that had to be handled was the jibsheets. Sometimes all hands would run forward to do that, the helmsman leaving the wheel in a becket with helm hard-a-lee. Of course, all but the spanker topsail would previously have been clewed. When we reefed a sail it would be lowered down on deck; the operation of tying in the reef was about like baling a carpet. The reef points were three-inch manila. All these activities were supervised personally by the skipper, who was kept thin running the length of her two-hundred-foot deck. He would even let go the anchor with his own hands.

This may not sound exciting, but one has only to be on one of these big vessels when wind and sea take command to witness action-a-plenty. One skipper I know was coming out of the Bay of Fundy in midwinter two years ago when, about off Schoodig, he ran into a northwest gale with snow. He had recently come up from Norfolk with a negro crew, and these men were useless in face of the bitter cold. The master, mate and donkey-engineer managed to get the spanker down before things froze up. After that they were helpless. The skipper and mate alternated at the wheel, hoping to make a lee and anchor in some Maine port, but the wind headed them and drove them back to sea. During the night all canvas except the furled spanker blew away. The three white men made shift to reef that and set it, but it too blew out before the vessel had time to round head to wind. The mate was injured and the donkey-man had both hands frozen, so the master steered her under bare poles across the Gulf of Maine and brought her to anchor in Yarmouth Road, Nova Scotia, with no help from the others on board. This is what happens when through bad judgment or bad luck sail is not shortened in time. The vessel was undamaged.

But my queerest experience in a coaster was entering a little New Brunswick port. After a dozen years of knocking round in small fore-and-aft rigged vessels one has certain ideas of how standard maneuvers should be performed, and in this case mine were all knocked galleywest. We were approaching the entrance with a fresh breeze over our port quarter when the skipper ordered the spanker lowered. The little harbor within was quite narrow and I wondered how in the world he would be able to round up in time without the aid of the spanker; but he grinned and told me the thing to look out for was that the spanker did not "take charge" and round her to against your will in shallow water with the wind aft. This was lesson number one. I was at the wheel and had a few rather nervous minutes: there was a big ground swell heaving in across the bar and in this the ship exhibited a strong tendency to round-to. At the same time she seemed to sag off bodily towards a series of ugly ledges under our lee, and between the two I had plenty of exercise trying to keep her in the fairway.

The skipper meantime had gone forward to superintend hauling down the jibs. This struck me as queer but later I realized that that was the business end of the ship. Although no effort was made to secure them it took a few minutes just to drag the four big headsails down, and I was all the time growing more and more anxious since we were dashing across the harbor at a lively pace and it did not look as though there was going to be room to round up. Surreptitiously I eased off a little so as to give more room to shoot, but the skipper instantly noticed the change and waved me back on my course. When we were right in the middle—just about where it seemed to me the anchor should have gone—he waved me quite nonchalantly to put my helm a-lee. I took one look at the forested, clifty shore scarcely a cable-length to windward and shied like a frightened horse. But there was no mistaking his signals, so gritting my teeth and looking the other way I jammed the helm hard down.

She responded promptly, and at the same time there came a tremendous roar: the "old man" had let go the port anchor. However, the chain ran out un-checked and I still had visions of laying her forefoot on the rocks as she continued to round up. But presently her sails started to shake and as they did so her head-way diminished very fast. As she lost way, of course, she ceased to turn, so the up-shot was that she came to rest in a few moments with the wind abeam — and never did actually come up into the wind at all.

Letting the anchor go was not the answer: that was done merely to range out the chain which otherwise would have lain in a heap on the bottom. The ship was so deep and her skin friction so great that despite the tremendous momentum of her loaded hull she was bound to check as soon as the power propelling her was removed. The skipper knew this and was not at all worried about the cliffs to windward, so near. He knew she would merely spill the wind and stop. But I did not, and I called that lesson number two in the art of handling a big fore-and-aft rigged freighter. I was destined to learn several more before the voyage was done.

# *Lines and Sail Plans*

My father was a skillful wood carver, and I remember a period of several weekends when I watched him transform a block of seasoned white pine into a beautiful little clipper-bowed hull about fourteen inches long. With the finished hull sitting in a pile of fragrant wood chips, he said that he would rig her as a square-rigged ship and give her to me. Naturally I was pleased, but the weeks went by, and nothing happened. When I asked when she would be finished, all my father would say was that the spars and rigging on a full-rigged ship were difficult to make and that he as yet hadn't had time to get to it. It must have been months later when I suggested that he make the hull into a schooner.

To my surprise and pleasure, he agreed, and then, working on Saturdays, he fashioned a bowsprit with a jibboom, a carved billet head, masts and topmasts, booms with goosenecks, gaffs, hatches, and a deckhouse with a real slide on the companionway. After a few weeks, he had made what, in my eyes, was the most perfect little coasting schooner imaginable, and this made his remark when he had finished totally incomprehensible to my young mind. Looking at her, he said, "She's the wrong shape for a schooner and no good at all. She was supposed to be a ship." It was as though all of a sudden he found himself finished with the detailed work that had taken his attention and emerged to look at what he had done.

Later, I understood what he meant, for she was deep with hard bilges, a broad counter, and a high, narrow rudder and had all the characteristics of a full-rigged downeaster. The lesson that a specific hull form demanded a specific rig was one that I have never forgotten.

On several occasions after that, my father and I walked about boats hauled out on ways and he would point out the entrance and the shape of the midship section and the run and show me how the form of a hull could be taken from a model and transformed to lines, which could be used to build a ship.

Most of the schooners in this book were probably built directly from models without using formal line drawings. The lines included here are intended only to give the reader a glimpse of the varied designs which are represented by the collection of vessels in the photographs. They will totally satisfy neither historian nor model builder.

— Edward W. Smith, Jr.

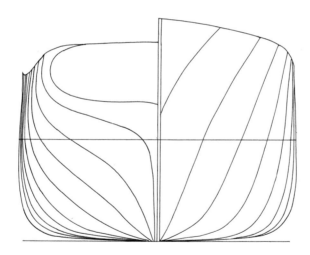

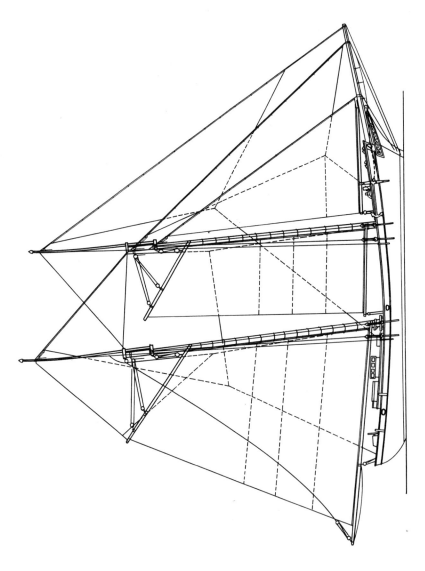

The sail plan of the *John Feeney*, the schooner shown in Plate 17. Note the tall, narrow foresail. This plan was drawn by the English naval architect and marine historian, John Leather, for his book, *Gaff Rig*.

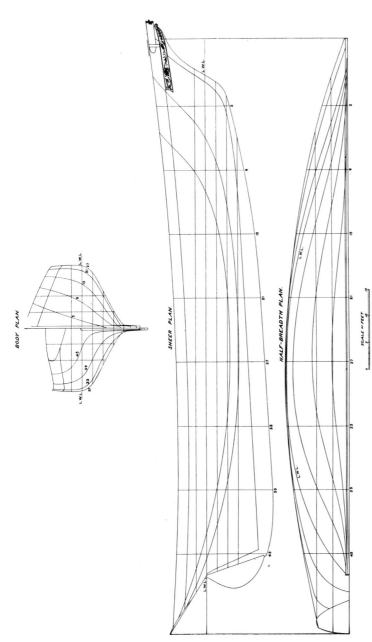

BODY PLAN

SHEER PLAN

HALF-BREADTH PLAN

SCALE IN FEET

The lines of the fishing schooner *Fredonia*. The story of this design created by the great yacht designer, Edward Burgess, as a logical development from his own experience has been told many times (see page 127). The *Fredonia* and her near sistership, the *Nellie Dixon*, were launched in 1889. Though the *Nellie Dixon* went fishing right away, the *Fredonia* was sold to Malcolm Forbes, who used her as a yacht for a year. She then went fishing. The *Fredonia's* length at the rail was 110 feet, 6 inches; her length between perpendiculars was 99 feet, 7 inches; her beam, 23 feet, 7 inches; and her depth of hold, 10 feet, 4 inches. Her net tonnage was 109.44. These lines, from *The National Watercraft Collection*, are from a copy probably made from the plan drawn by Edward Burgess.

187

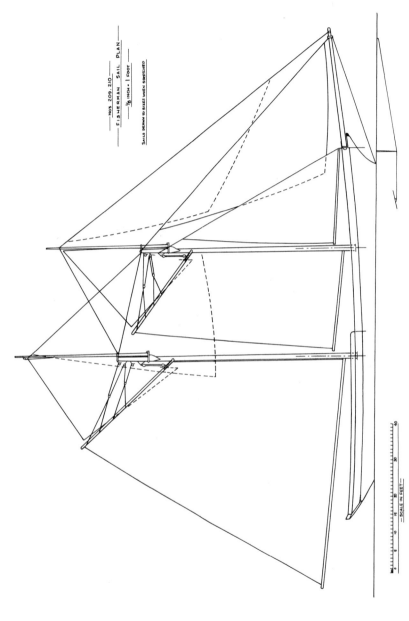

The sail plan for the *Harvard* and *Gloriana* shows a powerful rig for fast sailing in light and moderate breezes, yet one that is easily shortened down for heavy weather. Such versatility was, of course, an important advantage of the schooner rig and a significant reason for its great popularity for working vessels. The spar dimensions of these schooners were as follows: bowsprit, outboard, 33'9"; foremast, above the deck, 62'0"; fore topmast, 35'0"; mainmast, above deck, 68'9"; main topmast, 38'0"; main boom, 64'0"; main gaff, 34'6"; fore boom, 27'6"; fore gaff, 28'0". The plans of the *Harvard* were traced from drawings made as part of the *Historic American Merchant Marine Survey*.

188

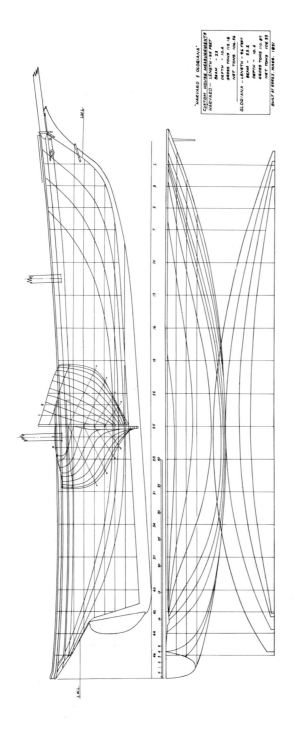

"HARVARD & GLORIANA"
CUSTOM HOUSE MEASUREMENTS
HARVARD— LENGTH - 95 FEET
BEAM - 23
DEPTH - 10.4
GROSS TONS 112.16
NET TONS 106.56

GLORIANA - LENGTH - 96 FEET
BEAM - 23.2
DEPTH - 10.4
GROSS TONS 110.87
NET TONS 105.53

BUILT AT ESSEX, MASS. 1891

The fishing schooners *Harvard* and *Gloriana* were both built to these lines, drawn by Edward Burgess. The design was not completed until after his death. The *Harvard* looks as though she could have carried a larger cargo and sailed nearly as fast as the *Fredonia*. She was a successful vessel and was in service until 1930. Her tonnage was 112 gross, 76 net. She was 95.4 feet long, 23.6 feet in beam, with a depth of 10.4 feet. (See Plate 40.)

189

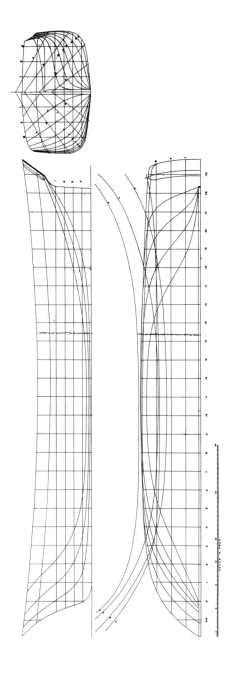

The lines of the schooner, *David Torrey*. She is a handsome vessel with graceful sheer, a pleasant flare at the bow, and a short and easy run. She had as nice a shape as any schooner you could find. She was designed and built by Richardson and Stubbs of Brunswick, Maine, for W. S. Jordan in 1873. Her moulded length was 102 feet, 10 inches; beam, 26 feet, 2 inches; and draft, 9 feet, 6 inches. Her gross tonnage was 166.05; net, 157.75. The *Torrey* is in the government registry until 1898, when she disappears without explanation. These lines were drawn for the *Historic American Merchant Marine Survey*.

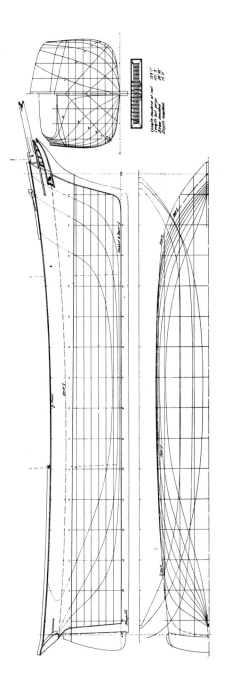

The lines of the brigantine, *J. W. Parker.* This is a deep-water vessel that may be compared to vessels such as the *Manson,* Plates 76, 77, and the *Starlight,* Plates 78, 79. The lines were drawn by Howard I. Chapelle from the builder's half-model and were published in *The National Watercraft Collection.*

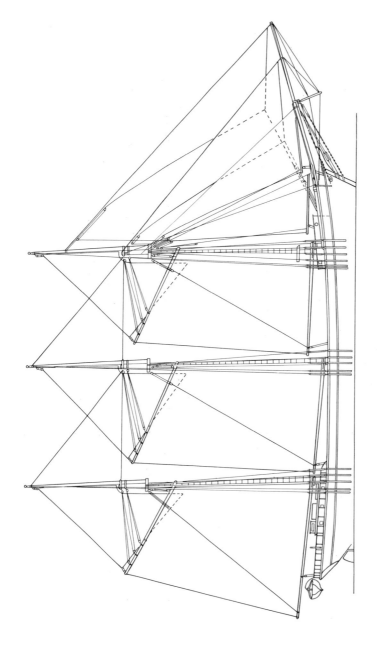

The sail plan of the three-masted, centerboard, coasting schooner, *William Bisbee*. Note that there is a club on the jib, as well as on the fore staysail, not an unusual arrangement in the larger schooners.

192

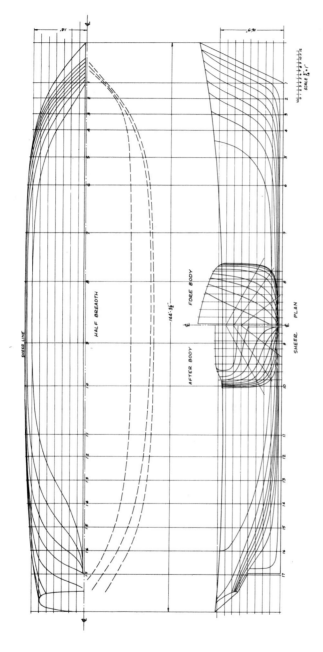

The lines of the *William Bisbee*. She was built in 1902 at Portland, Maine. She is typical of many three-masters built both before and after her launching date. The *Bisbee's* moulded length was 144 feet, 3-1/2 inches; her beam was 31 feet, 7 inches; and her draft, 8 feet, 6 inches. Her gross tonnage was 309; net tonnage, 206. She disappears from the registry in 1931. The plans of the *Bisbee* were traced from drawings made as part of the *Historic American Merchant Marine Survey*.

193

# Index of Vessels

*Index of Vessels in Plans* (by page number)

# THE FISHERMAN'S WAY

*[The men who sailed in fishing schooners were strong and spirited and used to a hard, adventurous life. The poem that follows gives an insight to a fisherman's life.]*

There haint no style on a fishin' craft,
No more than there is on a lumber raft,
The men of her crew berth fore and aft,
And ship on the self-same lay.
The rules, what there is, are fair and square,
"Each man is expected to do his share"
If he don't — waal, somebody parts his hair!
For that is the fisherman's way.

   In port, sometimes, when you're fittin' out,
   You kin hear men argue and growl and spout
   With the skipper, who, maybe, is watchin' out
   While they tauten a shroud er stay:
   "This here is a devilish rotten fall!"
   "That fore-s'l you got don't fit a-tall!"
   But the skipper says: "Heave ahead!" that's all.
   For that is the fisherman's way.

When the fleet stands out on the off-shore tack,
A-cartin' sail till the mastheads crack,
And there haint a line or a stay that's slack,
You will hear these fellows say:
"We're holdin' our own, without no fuss.
No son-of-a-gun takes the wind from us.
Our spars are springin'? They might do wuss!"
For that is the fisherman's way.

On the fishing bank when the trawls are set
Or the seine-boats out with a mile of net,
And the fog drops down like a blanket, wet,
That shuts out the light of day.
They don't stop to figure out which is worst,
To swamp and go down or die of thirst
But say, "Damn the man who gives in first!"
For that is the fisherman's way.

   When one of the fleet gets blown inshore,
   And strands on the rocks in the breakers' roar,
   You think that the rest dodge an extra chore?
   Or twiddle their hands and pray?
   It's: "Over the dories!" and off pell-mell,
   And as they shove clear you can hear em yell:
   "We'll fetch em all back or we'll go to hell!"
   For that is the fisherman's way.

So they live their lives all along our coast,
They suffer some, but their women, most,
But there's always one for to take his post
When a lad goes out to stay.
For the risk and toil and the miseree,
Can't scare a fisherman off the sea,
It was always so, and 'twill always be,
For that is the fisherman's way.

*Reprinted from* Martha's Vineyard Boats, *by Joseph C. Allen, by permission of the Dukes County Historical Society, Edgartown, Massachusetts*

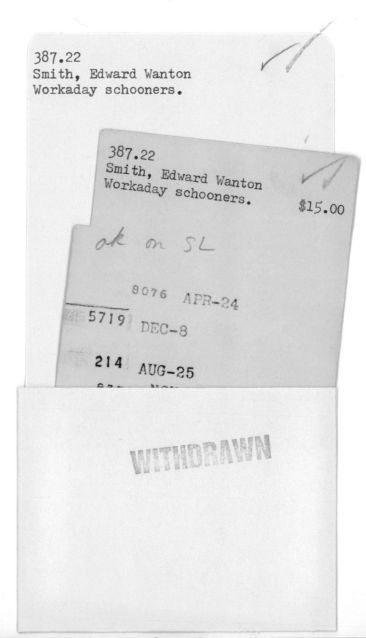

387.22
Smith, Edward Wanton
Workaday schooners.

387.22
Smith, Edward Wanton
Workaday schooners.

$15.00

ok on SL

8076 APR-24

5719 DEC-8

214 AUG-25